Gifts
for the
Marketplace

Gifts
for the
Marketplace

by R. L. Brandt

Christian Publishing Services, Inc.
Tulsa, Oklahoma

Gifts for the Marketplace
ISBN 0-88144-142-2
Copyright © 1989 by R. L. Brandt
1520 Westwood Drive
Billings, MT 59102

Published by Christian Publishing Services, Inc.
P. O. Box 55388
Tulsa, OK 74155-1388

Dedication

Lovingly dedicated
to
Marian
my beloved companion for nearly half
a century, whose loving, caring, and
dedicated Christian life has been
largely responsible for any worthwhile
thing I may have done.

Contents

Foreword

Preface

1 Gifts for the Marketplace   15

2 The Gifts and Acts 1:8   23

3 Imperatives   33

4 Motivation   51

5 The Selfsame Spirit   59

6 The Word of Wisdom   71

7 The Word of Knowledge   87

8 The Gift of Faith   105

9 Gifts of Healing   119

10 Working of Miracles   133

11 Prophecy   149

12 Discerning of Spirits   167

13 Divers Kinds of Tongues   179

14 Interpretation of Tongues   207

15 From the Meeting Place to the Marketplace   215

Bibliography   219

Foreword

The forces of darkness are making a fearsome onslaught on our world. The unleashing of the powers of hell gives evidence of the prevalent spirit of Antichrist. But Almighty God, the omnipotent One, has the antidote to this abounding sin. It is none other than the Holy Spirit.

The Church cannot cope with the world, the flesh and the devil apart from divine help. God's work cannot be effectively done except through the power of the Holy Spirit. (Zechariah 4:6.) "The only answer to the unleashed power of the enemy is the manifested power of God."

The winds of the Holy Spirit are freely and effectively blowing today. Never in history have so many people been affected by the phenomenon of the outpoured Spirit. Millions testify to a personal Pentecost. Members of denominations large and small have experienced manifestations of the Spirit.

The moving of the Spirit around the world has created great interest. Much is being preached and written on the subject. There is a need for a Scriptural understanding of what God is doing, a need to have an "understanding of the times, to know what...to do" (1 Chronicles 12:32).

R. L. Brandt gives us a thoughtful and challenging exposition on the manifestations of the Spirit. The subject is not new. Many have written on it, but the author of *Gifts for the Marketplace* has a way of making order and good sense out of a complex study. Readers will find a refreshingly new approach to the whole field of spiritual gifts.

Our understanding of the gifts of the Spirit and their purpose is vital. These manifestations are flashes of God's omniscience and omnipotence shown supernaturally through His followers.

The gifts of the Spirit are God's intended norm for His Church. But they are not only for His Body when engaged in corporate worship, they are also for the marketplace. That is where they were prominent in the Early Church.

The image of God, as revealed through the operation of the Spirit's gifts, touched the marketplace in Apostolic days and can and must do the same today.

My longtime and cherished friend, R. L. Brandt, has written this lucid and concise book toward that end.

G. Raymond Carlson
General Superintendent
Assemblies of God

Preface

Thomas A. Smail, in his illuminating book, *The Forgotten Father*, notes that "within the (Charismatic) renewal there has been an obsession with personal experience and sometimes even with trivial providences at the expense of the call to evangelize and act amidst the needs of society, which is perhaps understandable in the early stages of a renewal movement, but which becomes disconcerting when it continues after many years."[1] And Dr. E. V. Hill, pastor of Mount Zion Missionary Baptist Church in Los Angeles, California, addressing the 1984 Conference on the Holy Spirit in Springfield, Missouri, astutely observed that the gifts of the Spirit are not for franchising, nor for colonizing, but for evangelizing.

From my own vantage point it appears that the Pentecostal world has generally held the view that the function of the Spirit's gifts is to be essentially fulfilled within the four walls of the sanctuary where the Body of Christ is assembled. I have heard of churches wherein all nine of the gifts spoken of by Paul in 1 Corinthians 12:8-10 have been reportedly manifested. Yet, while I rejoice over every genuine manifestation of these gifts, wherever it occurs, I, in consequence of a rather careful examination of the gifts in the Early Church, have been alerted to the rather startling fact that the earliest, and at least somewhat precedential manifestations of the gifts, were more commonly in the marketplace rather than in the meeting place. And also that while a few of the gifts, particularly tongues, interpretation of tongues, and prophecy, are designated for edification of the Body while it is met together, they also have an important evangelizing function. Certainly, tongues-speaking, though it is essentially a worship gift and thus very much in order in the assembly, has also an evangelization significance: **Wherefore tongues are for a sign, not to them that believe, but to them that believe not...**(1 Cor. 14:22).

And while the gift of prophecy is for the edification, exhortation and comfort of the Body, it, too, may serve as a very meaningful means of evangelization:

> **But if all prophesy, and there come in one that believeth not, or one unlearned, he is convinced of all, he is judged of all:**
>
> **And thus are the secrets of his heart made manifest; and so falling down on his face he will worship God, and report that God is in you of a truth.**
>
> **1 Corinthians 14:24,25**

A totally new and exciting perspective emerges when we begin to understand that the gifts can serve a most meaningful purpose in the marketplace. By "marketplace" I mean the arena wherein we rub shoulders with humanity. I mean such places as outside the temple gate (Acts 3:1-11); in the court room (Acts 4:5-12); in the city streets (Acts 5:12-16); inside prison walls (Acts 5:18-21); on the mission field (Acts 8:5-8); on the road to Gaza (Acts 8:26-40); in the bedroom of the afflicted (Acts 9:32-35); in the "morgue" (Acts 9:36-41); on the housetop (Acts 10:9-21); in the home of the spiritually hungry (Acts 10:23-48); and in many other such places.

In this book I intend to take a new look at all nine of the gifts listed by Paul in 1 Corinthians 12:8-10. But beyond that, I will endeavor to share some insights relating to the whole field of the Spirit's gifts which heretofore have not been in focus —- at least not in my focus.

R. L. B.

Notes

[1]Thomas A. Smail, *The Forgotten Father* (Grand Rapids: William B. Eerdmans Publishing Co., 1980), p. 15.

1

Gifts for the Marketplace

During the summer and fall of 1988, large sections of Montana and Wyoming, including Yellowstone National Park, were struck by devastating forest and prairie fires, the worst in 200 years, it has been reported. Numerous homes were destroyed, herds of livestock threatened, vast timberlands wiped out, and hundreds of thousands of acres of forest and grasslands blackened. High winds carried the flames unrelentingly through the tinder-dry hills and valleys, despite the valiant efforts of the largest army of trained firefighters ever amassed in the two states.

One of the devices used in combating the gigantic blaze was the deliberate setting of back fires. The idea was to fight fire with fire. A fire might be racing through the forest, jumping roads and firelines, destroying everything in its path. Firefighters would get ahead of the flames, perhaps to a road which crossed the path of the oncoming blaze. They would start a new fire in the tinder-dry grass and trees on the side toward which the fire was burning. The new blaze would burn back against the wind toward the approaching inferno. When the big fire reached the already burned area, it found no more fuel to feed upon and naturally died.

There is, in this situation, a profound spiritual lesson for the Church. She, too, must learn to fight fire with fire.

The enemy has started a lot of "fires" in our world; that is his business: **The thief cometh not, but for to steal, and to kill, and to destroy...**(John 10:10). On every hand, raging "fires" seem to be burning out of control, leaving awful devastation in their wake.

Our world is experiencing an unprecedented invasion of darkness. Godlessness threatens to dominate society. Humanism infests and infects every nook and cranny of our culture. Satanism increases at an alarming rate. Occultism, with its subtle fascination, holds many in its demonic grip. Wholesale murder by abortion has become a way of life. Divorce, broken homes, and family disintegration are a national phenomenon which defies the imagination. Homosexuality has become an accepted "alternate lifestyle," and those who practice it loudly and boldly demand equal rights with the rest of society. Child abuse has reached unbelievable proportions. Pornography is brashly foisted upon the public, polluting the minds of both the young and the not-so-young. Eastern religions and strange cults proliferate. Alcoholism and drug abuse bind and blind millions. Sexual immorality invades the Church to a shocking degree. Communism knocks unrelentingly at our doors. And there is a prevailing climate, as in Israel in the days of Elijah the prophet, in which people wonder just who is God.

What does all of this have to do with the gifts of the Spirit? Why focus on such negative conditions? The answer is quite simple. The gifts of the Spirit are not for mere spiritual entertainment, nor for theological speculation. They are intended for very practical everyday application in the midst of the world at large. They are designed for both defense and offense. They are to encourage, edify, and equip the saints, and at the same time they are to support the Church's invasion into enemy territory on behalf of world evangelization.

Without a doubt the Church's priority need of the hour is a revival of the gifts of the Spirit. It was the supernatural manifestation in Elijah's time, in his calling down fire from heaven, that launched a new day for Israel. Should we doubt that supernatural manifestations today would be any less effective?

Tucked away in 1 Chronicles 12:32 is a powerful line for our encouragement. Regarding the children of Issachar, we are told that they ...**were men that had understanding of times, to know what Israel ought to do**....

Can we not rightly conclude, in the light of this revelation, that God will grant us, His children who earnestly seek Him today, an understanding of our times so we will know what to do?

Need we be reminded that ...**we wrestle not against flesh and blood, but against principalities, against powers, against the rulers of the darkness of this world, against spiritual wickedness in high places** (Eph. 6:12)? It is imperative that this truth be taken seriously, for here the Church's prime enemy is identified. "Our conflict is not with men here denoted by 'flesh and blood', which is usually a symbol of weakness, therefore denoting that our opponents are not weak mortals, but powers of a far more formidable order."[1]

In the midst of an educated, sophisticated society, there is a tendency to overlook the real foe, and instead to attribute our conflicts to "flesh and blood" (that is, to heredity, to social conditions, to environment, to political entities, and to other rationalized forces).

While we may decry the popular "the-devil-made-me-do-it" syndrome, we dare not swing so far to the other extreme that we lose sight of the very real forces of darkness against whom our warfare is waged. Paul makes it clear that our conflict is with invisible spiritual entities whose influence is worldwide, whose kingdom is "darkness," and whose whole object is to destroy the Church and to dethrone God.

Thus the question is: How does the Church cope, both defensively and offensively, in the face of this invading, destroying enemy? For the answer to that question, we need look no further than to Paul:

> **For though we walk in the flesh, we do not war after the flesh:**
>
> **(For the weapons of our warfare are not carnal, but mighty through God to the pulling down of strong holds;)**
>
> **Casting down imaginations, and every high thing that exalteth itself against the knowledge of God, and bringing into captivity every thought to the obedience of Christ.**
>
> **2 Corinthians 10:3-5**

The Christian's warfare is not in the realm of the flesh, nor should it be thought that the battle may be won by the flesh (that is, by purely human and natural weapons, be they ever so clever and sharply honed).

The unmistakable message of human history is that the only effective answer to the unleashed power of the enemy is the manifested power of God: **So shall they fear the name of the Lord from the west, and his glory**

from the rising of the sun. When the enemy shall come in like a flood, the Spirit of the Lord shall lift up a standard against him (Is. 59:19). **...This is the word of the Lord..., Not by might, nor by power, but by my spirit, saith the Lord of hosts** (Zech. 4:6).

I fear the Church is too often seduced by the world system and by ecclesiastical intellectuality toward dependence upon "the arm of flesh." We are subtly tempted to "go down to Egypt for help" instead of resorting to the weapons "which are mighty through God to the pulling down of strong holds."

We do well to ask ourselves again: How did the Early Church score so highly in the face of the overwhelming odds against it? There is but a single, very obvious answer — they were full of the Holy Ghost. Let the record speak for itself: **Then Peter, filled with the Holy Ghost, said...**(Acts 4:8); **...and they chose Stephen, a man full of faith and of the Holy Ghost...**(Acts 6:5); **For he was a good man, and full of the Holy Ghost and of faith: and much people was added unto the Lord** (Acts 11:24); **Then Saul,...filled with the Holy Ghost, set his eyes on him, And said...**(Acts 13:9,10).

Thank God, a new day is dawning for the Church. On the spiritual horizon a "cloud the size of a man's hand" is rising. Some believe we are on the threshold of the mightiest manifestation of God's power through the gifts of the Spirit since the launching of the Church in the first century.

Recent events certainly lend credence to that idea. I will cite a single example here and will demonstrate it more fully throughout the succeeding chapters.

For nearly a decade the pastor of a large church in Oregon felt constrained to spend considerable time waiting on the Lord. Out of this time of prayer and meditation came some remarkable manifestations of spiritual gifts.

One night, while the pastor was quietly waiting upon the Lord, preparing his heart for ministry in the evening service, he sensed the voice of God addressing him: "In the service tonight will be a person who has committed murder. It was done with a 38-caliber service revolver. This person has not been able to experience self-forgiveness, though the time has been served. I want this person to accept My forgiveness and know My love."

Taken aback by such a strange word, the pastor wondered if his imagination was working overtime, or whether he had really received a word of knowledge by the Spirit.

Soon it was time for the service to begin. The singing was already in progress. All this time the pastor was struggling to push the strange word from his mind. But to no avail.

Again, during a period of prayer and worship, he wrestled with the idea of declaring his revelation to the congregation. "After all," he reasoned, "I am the pastor and I'm not leaving town tomorrow. I'm going to have to live with my words." Nevertheless, the idea clung to his mind along with the gentle constraint to declare it.

Finally he decided on a course of action. Standing before the congregation, he carefuly set the stage for his strange message. "This could be just plain me," he announced, "but I really feel it is the Spirit of God." He went on to state that he did not want anyone to raise a hand or stand up, but he felt he must share the strange word, which he then proceeded to do.

It wasn't the easiest service for preaching, for a silent spell seemed to hang over the place like a cloud. It is easy to imagine people glancing over their shoulders and from side to side, secretly wondering, "Am I sitting next to a murderer?"

Following the message, a crowd gathered around the altar for a time of more than ordinary prayer. Finally it was over, and most of the congregation had departed. The pastor was going around turning off the lights when a lady approached him asking if she could have a word with him, to which he agreed.

"But I'd like to speak with you in private, if I may," she requested.

"Come into my office," the pastor invited.

In the quietness of his office, she told her story. "I am a stranger in your city. I moved here six months ago, and I work at Sacred Heart Hospital."

She went on to say: "This is my first time in your church. No one here knows me. But today I felt constrained to come here. And in my first service you told my story just as it is.

"I lived in the eastern part of the U.S. with my husband and children. My husband was a policeman, but he was also a drinker. On a Christmas eve he came home intoxicated, threatening to beat our 13-year-old daughter. He had done this to my two children and me so many times before that I could no longer bear it. So I went to the bedroom, took his 38-caliber service revolver from the bureau drawer, went to the living room and shot him. He fell dead under the Christmas tree.

"For this I went to prison and served my time. While there I found the Lord, but from the time of that awful event until now I have not been able to escape a dark, evil kind of conscience. I have never known a day of peace.

"But tonight I came here, and without knowing me, you told my story just as it happened. When you said, 'You are forgiven, and God wants you to know He loves you,' it was as if that cloud gathered itself up and lifted, and tonight I am free!"

The pastor reports that the lady became a radiant Christian, later joined his church and married a fine man. She and her husband have moved to another city, but she continues to lead a beautiful Christian life.

Notes

[1]The Rev. Professor W. G. Blaikie, D.D., *The Pulpit Commentary on Ephesians*, Wartime edition (London and New York: Funk and Wagnalls Company), p. 258.

2
The Gifts and Acts 1:8

But ye shall receive power coming the Holy Spirit upon you, and ye shall be of me witnesses both in Jerusalem and in all Judea and Samaria and unto extremity of the earth.

Acts 1:8[1]

The time has arrived for the Body of Christ to recognize that the gifts of the Spirit are God's intended norm for His Church. There are discernable reasons for the total lack of such manifestations in some quarters, and for the minimal manifestations, at best, in other quarters.

On the one hand, certain theologians, especially the devoted dispensationalists, have vigorously insisted that at least some of the gifts were only temporary endowments for getting the Church launched. And, at the same time, they have de-emphasized the supernatural to such an extent that the faith of their disciples for any of the gifts is almost non-existent. Where faith is lacking, there also the gifts will not appear.

And, on the other hand, even where the gifts are acknowledged, and the supernatural is not spurned, there have been minimal manifestations, and that for a number of rather obvious reasons.

While there is now an apparent Spirit-quickened desire for the gifts, there is also a prevailing ignorance which imposes its own severe limitations. Ignorance seems always to be the problem. It was the problem at Corinth, as Paul noted in his letter to the believers there: **Now concerning spiritual gifts, brethren, I would not have you ignorant** (1 Cor. 12:1). It is no doubt our problem too. But there is a hopeful sign. People want to know.

My book *Charismatics, Are We Missing Something?*[2] has an appendix wherein I provided a five-step sequence of events related to historical outpourings of the Holy Spirit. It will be helpful to repeat this sequence of events and make a comment.

1. Evident spiritual hunger (on the part of men and women).

2. Outpouring of the Holy Spirit (God's response).

3. Manifestation of the gifts of the Spirit.

4. Abuse and/or misuse of the gifts.

5. Correction or disintegration.

Abuse and/or misuse of the gifts has often dampened enthusiasm for them. While this situation is understandable, it is also unfortunate. Abuses and misuses commonly spring from ignorance. Thus it is vital that a base of Spirit-inspired biblical knowledge be established. Only when this is accomplished will the God-intended norm for the Church be achieved.

Again, due to the rather widespread lack of knowledge regarding the divine intention for the gifts, they are often relegated to a place of little importance. Or, at best, the Body gets "hung up on" the utterance gifts and loses sight of all others.

There is another related reason for lack of spiritual gifts. It may well be the chief reason. It is the everlasting tendency for Spirit-filled believers to slip into a state of spiritual dormancy. If it could happen to the able young preacher Timothy, and to believers at Ephesus, it may easily happen to all. Paul's admonition to Timothy was **...stir up the gift of God, which is in thee by the putting on of my hands** (2 Tim. 1:6). And to the Ephesians he urged, **...be filled with the Spirit** (Eph. 5:18). This latter exhortation could be better translated, "be *being* filled with the Spirit."

In the light of what we have already noted, it is our intention to pursue, throughout the remainder of this book, a better understanding of the whole matter of spiritual gifts.

Acts 1:8 is a vital point from which to launch our quest. Before us are the words of our Lord, deserving the most thoughtful consideration: **...ye shall receive power after that the Holy Ghost is come upon you: and ye shall be witnesses unto me....** It is extremely easy to miss the whole point of the Master's message, especially when "and ye shall be witnesses unto me" is perceived as a commandment akin to the Great Commission. Of utmost importance is recognition of the fact that in this verse there is no element of command whatsoever. Instead there is a declaration of two notable facts; or to state it another way, proclamation of two inevitable consequences of the coming of the Spirit.

First is the almost electrifying fact that Jesus said that in consequence of the Spirit's coming upon believers, they would experience a power unknown to them. The word *power* in this verse is a translation of the Greek word *dunamis*, which means "force," and even more specifically "miraculous power" (usually by implication a miracle itself). The source of the power was to be the Holy Spirit Himself. Thus it must be perceived to be nothing less than God's own power. We do well to ponder this truth deeply for herein lies the secret of the Church's most effective offensive and defensive action. Without this miraculous power, the Church is as weak as mere men. With it, the Church is invincible.

The second fact, "and ye shall be witnesses unto me" is totally dependent upon the first fact, "ye shall receive power after that the Holy Ghost is come upon you." The witness and the power are inseparable. The power is supernatural, and the witness is likewise supernatural. Without supernatural power, there can be no supernatural witness.

What do we mean by "supernatural witness"? We mean that form of witness so evident in the Early Church beyond Acts 2:4. We mean that witness which involved manifestation of the mighty power of God: **And with great power gave the apostles witness of the resurrection of the Lord Jesus...**(Acts 4:33).

The power promised in Acts 1:8 was experienced initially and personally in Acts 2:4, and it was manifested gloriously throughout the remainder of the book of Acts.

In what form did the newfound power find its expression? Was it simply that the early believers proclaimed the Gospel with more boldness and persuasiveness than ever before, or was there some other element which needs to be discovered? That the Gospel was preached with more boldness and persuasiveness is unquestionable. Nonetheless, there was another element, ever present but too easily overlooked. It is the remarkable manifestation of the spiritual gifts which in a very real and unmistakable sense constituted the witness of which Jesus spoke in Acts 1:8.

The Early Church perceived the connection between the bold proclamation of the Gospel and the manifestation of the Spirit's gifts. Listen to the prayer of these early disciples:

> ...and grant unto thy servants, that with all boldness they may speak thy word,
>
> By stretching forth thine hand to heal; and that signs and wonders may be done by the name of thy holy child Jesus.
>
> **Acts 4:29,30**

They understood that supernatural gifts manifested through them would transform them into effective witnesses unto Christ. Do we understand that truth?

A survey of the book of Acts beyond Acts 2:4 reveals a constant and consistent manifestation of the supernatural through the believers by way of spiritual gifts. As many as eighty or more manifestations of gifts can be identified.

In a moment we will journey through the book of Acts, beginning with Acts 2:4, for the express purpose of ferreting out manifestations of the gifts. However, another observation is important before we launch our search. It is that we will discover a mingling of the gifts, so much so that at times we may question just which gift (or gifts) is being manifested. This need cause us no real concern, for it must be remembered that all of the gifts flow from the identical source, the Holy Spirit. If we are unable to identify exactly and classify perfectly, let us not be overly concerned. As humans it is our nature to draw neat lines of separation and classification, but when we seek to impose this practice upon God, we only frustrate ourselves, and we may generate unnecessary confusion.

We now launch our survey of the book of Acts, chapter by chapter, in our quest for evidence of manifested gifts.

1. Acts 2:4 — gift of tongues
   2:8-11 — gift of miracles (Note: here is possibly the first instance of mingling of gifts. Not only was there tongues-speaking, but that men spoke languages unknown to them was indeed a miracle.)
   2:14-36 — gift of prophecy
   2:23 — word of wisdom

2. Acts 3:1-11 — gift of faith
   — gifts of healing
   — gift of miracles (see Acts 4:16-22)
   3:12-26 — gift of prophecy
   — possibly word of wisdom

3. Acts 4:8-12 — gift of prophecy
   4:31 — possibly gift of miracles
   4:33 — other gifts, but not identified

4. Acts 5:3-10 — discerning of spirits
— word of knowledge
— word of wisdom
— working of miracles
     5:15 — working of miracles
     5:16 — gifts of healing
     5:19 — working of miracles

5. Acts 6:10 — word of wisdom

6. Acts 7:2-53 — gift of prophecy
     7:55,56 — possibly word of knowledge

7. Acts 8:7 — gifts of healing
     8:22 — word of knowledge
     8:23 — discerning of spirits
     8:39 — working of miracles

8. Acts 9:10-12 — word of knowledge
     9:17,18 — gifts of healing
— possibly gift of faith
     9:34 — gifts of healing
— gift of faith
— working of miracles
     9:40 — gift of faith
— working of miracles

9. Acts 10:10-16 — word of wisdom
     10:19-21 — word of knowledge
     10:34-44 — gift of prophecy
     10:46 — gift of tongues

10. Acts 11:27-30 — gift of prophecy

11. Acts 13:2 — word of knowledge
— possibly gift of prophecy
     13:9-11 — discerning of spirits
— word of knowledge

- —working of miracles
- —possibly word of wisdom

12. Acts 14:3 — unidentified gifts
    14:9 — discerning of spirits, or word of knowledge
    14:10 — working of miracles
    — gifts of healing
    14:20 — working of miracles

13. Acts 15:5-22 — word of wisdom
    15:32 — possibly word of wisdom

14. Acts 16:6-10 — word of knowledge
    — possibly word of wisdom
    16:16-18 — discerning of spirits
    — working of miracles
    16:25,26 — working of miracles

15. Acts 17:22-31 — possibly gift of prophecy

16. Acts 18:9,10 — word of knowledge

17. Acts 19:2 — possibly discerning of spirits
    19:6 — gift of tongues
    — gift of prophecy
    19:11 — working of miracles
    19:21 — word of knowledge

18. Acts 20:2 — possibly gift of prophecy
    20:10 — working of miracles
    20:23 — word of knowledge
    20:29 — word of knowledge

19. Acts 21:4 — possibly tongues, prophecy, word of knowledge, or word of wisdom

    21:11 — gift of prophecy
    — word of knowledge

20. Acts 22:17-21—word of knowledge
21. Acts 23:11   — word of knowledge
22. Acts 24:25   —possibly word of wisdom
23. Acts 26:1-32 —possibly gift of prophecy
            —possibly word of wisdom
24. Acts 27:21-26—word of knowledge
      27:31   —word of wisdom
25. Acts 28:5   —working of miracles
      28:8,9 —gifts of healing

With such an impressive list, we can be confident that the gifts of the Spirit were of enormous consequence to the Early Church. Without the constant manifestation of those gifts, the Church would have faltered and failed, and the world would have been the poorer for it. But with them, not only did the Church prosper within itself and influence the nations and generations which it immediately touched, but it was to leave its imprint upon every succeeding generation, even until today.

Notes

[1]*Zondervan Parallel New Testament in Greek and English* (Grand Rapids: Zondervan Publishing Company, 1980), p. 343.

[2]R. L. Brandt, *Charismatics, Are We Missing Something?* (Plainfield: Logos International, 1981), p. 127. Distributed by Bridge Publications, Inc., 2500 Hamilton Blvd., S. Plainfield, NJ 07080.

3

Imperatives

Since the Spirit's gifts are intended for such high purposes — edification of those within the Church and ministry to human need, including evangelization of those outside the Church — it is our duty and responsibility to discover the most effective means to their meaningful manifestation.

To get us moving in that direction, I cite my parable of the sprinkler system.

During the summer of 1979 my wife and I built a house on a pie-shaped lot at the end of a dead-end street in Billings, Montana. We designed the house ourselves and managed the building project, including the landscaping.

When it was finally finished, we had a sizable yard, several flower beds and a rather large garden area. However, at that point, we confronted a problem. Billings tends to have a rather dry climate. Thus, raising a lush lawn, beautiful flowers, and a productive garden requires artificial watering. And city water is very costly. We could envision water bills large enough to discourage all horticultural interests and pursuits.

Nevertheless, there was a possible solution to the problem — a well of our own. So we engaged a well digger. He set up his rig about six feet from the end of the house. At a depth of approximately 23 feet, he struck a veritable lake. The supply of water was so abundant that several neighbors had their own wells dug.

Now in that vast reservoir was exactly what the lawn, flower beds and garden required. All that was needed was a means of transporting the water from its source to the areas of need. This called for the installation of a well casing and a pumping system to bring the supply to the level of need. Beyond that, a sprinkler system would distribute the water to the respective areas to be covered.

However, when the system became operable, I discovered another obstacle. The main devices for distributing the water properly were the sprinkler heads. All too easily they would get fouled with fine sand, causing the flow through them to be reduced to a mere trickle — little more than enough to keep the head itself wet. Or, on occasion, a sprinkler head would get stuck, resulting in the spray covering only a sliver of that particular sprinkler's intended field. In each instance the solution was to flush the sand from the head so it could function freely.

What a picture of the Spirit's gifts. There is a vast reservoir — God Himself — in which resides exactly what man needs for his spiritual flourishing. Howbeit, as long as the "water" remains in the Great Reservoir, regardless of how effective it might be if it reached the field, it is of little consequence at the point of need.

Therefore, the principal concern is transportation of the supply from the source to the point of demand and need. In the case of my yard, the water had first to be brought to ground level. This is exactly what our Lord did when He gave the Holy Spirit: **Therefore**

being by the right hand of God exalted, and having received of the Father the promise of the Holy Ghost, he hath shed forth this, which ye now see and hear (Acts 2:33).

Like the well casing and pump, the Holy Spirit brings the supply from the Great Reservoir to the level of the need. Even so, that is not enough. The supply must be distributed. The means to this end for my yard was the sprinkler system, particularly the heads; whereas God's means is Spirit-filled believers.

Here I should note that my sprinkler system was of little value apart from the life-giving substance it was designed to distribute. The real answer was in the water, and the sprinkler system took on tremendous meaning only as it carried that water. The spiritual lesson is self-evident.

The sprinkler system, especially the heads, equates with believers through whom God intends to impart of Himself on behalf of the field of mankind. Just as the sprinklers alone are not the answer to the lawn's need, so believers, important as they are, are not an adequate answer to the needs of their fellowman. The only answer is that which is in the Great Reservoir. Nothing less will suffice.

And, even as the major distribution problem in my system lay in the sprinkler heads, the major problem in the application of God Himself to the needs of man lies in us who are believers. Dare I say it? We have "sand" in our "heads"! At one time we may have been Spirit-filled to the point of which Jesus spoke when He said of the person who believes on him, **. . .out of his belly shall flow rivers of living water** (John 7:38), but now there remains only a trickle, barely enough to water ourselves. Or perhaps the "head" is stuck so that we concentrate on only a few gifts of the Spirit — perhaps the utterance gifts — at the expense of all the others, and as a result only a sliver of the field's real need is being touched.

How then can we assure the kind of gifts manifestation so direly needed in our world? How can we get the "sand" out of our "heads" so that supply and demand may be beautifully joined?

At the outset let us be reminded that the Holy Spirit has been given; the supply has been delivered to the level of the field. At one point in history this was not the case. All men could not receive the Holy Spirit: **(...the Holy Ghost was not yet given; because that Jesus was not yet glorified)** (John 7:39). But all of that changed on the momentous day of Pentecost. Then and there the Holy Ghost Who "was not yet given" was poured out upon the earth. He was made available to all: **For the promise is unto you, and to your children, and to all that are afar off, even as many as the Lord our God shall call** (Acts 2:39).

Now all men (and women) may be filled with the Spirit, and when this occurs, the potential for any and all of the Spirit's gifts is immediate:

> **And it shall come to pass in the last days, saith God, I will pour out of my Spirit upon all flesh: and your sons and your daughters shall prophesy, and your young men shall see visions, and your old men shall dream dreams:**
>
> **And on my servants and on my handmaidens I will pour out in those days of my Spirit; and they shall prophesy.**
>
> **Acts 2:17,18**

Therefore we conclude that if the Spirit's gifts are to bless the field today, there is a single prerequisite: **...be filled with the Spririt** (Eph. 5:18).

We must understand, too, that when a believer is filled with the Spirit, all of the properties of the Spirit are in him. To state it another way, the Spirit's gifts are resident in the Spirit Himself. Therefore when the believer becomes Spirit-filled, all of the gifts are resident in him. Once this truth is clearly perceived, it eliminates the need for conferral of gifts, as was the practice of the Latter Rain Movement about the middle of this century.

Although there is potential for manifestation of any and all gifts of the Spirit in a single believer, it is not likely this will happen, for **...all these worketh that one and the selfsame Spirit, dividing to every man severally as he will** (1 Cor. 12:11).

An individual's circumstances, temperament, faith, willingness, and particular ministry will certainly have a bearing upon the gifts which may be manifested through him. For example, ministry gifts will likely be more often evidenced through one who is in a position where more gifts of the Spirit may be meaningfully manifested than through one who is confined to the role of housewife or farmer. This is not in any way to infer that housewives and farmers cannot be used in manifesting gifts of the Spirit, for they most certainly can, but I speak of general opportunity and occasion.

The question now arises: Why, if it is true that the Spirit's gifts are manifested through Spirit-filled people, do we not see more gifts manifested? And, when gifts are manifested, why are they usually just the utterance gifts?

Let's consider the last question first. One reason for the commonality of utterance gifts in the congregation is their generality of application. Through these gifts the entire congregation may be edified. Their essential function seems to be indicated for those assembled together: **...when ye come together, every one of you hath a psalm, hath a doctrine, hath a tongue, hath a revelation, hath an interpretation. Let all things be done unto edifying** (1 Cor. 14:26). While the utterance gifts are most common in the meeting place, they should, by their edifying force, prepare the people for the marketplace where the other gifts may be most meaningfully manifested.

As to why we do not see more gifts manifested through Spirit-filled people, there are several obvious reasons. I will list three, and then consider each separately:

1. Those who experience the infilling of the Spirit have a tendency not to remain Spirit-filled.

2. There prevails a general lack of understanding regarding the gifts which militates against their manifestation.

3. There is a discernable neglect and failure to follow Paul's rather strong imperatives relating to the gifts.

From earliest times the Church has been cyclic in its spiritual fervor. There have been periods wherein believers flowed readily with the Spirit; and equally as often there have been periods of almost total unresponsiveness on the part of Christians. While there is not a lot of evidence of ebb and flow in the Early Church, there is a strong hint of it in Acts 4. The Holy Spirit was poured out upon the 120 in the upper room, as recorded in Acts 2, and ...**they were all filled with the Holy Ghost**...(v. 4). However, Acts 4:31 seems to indicate a later refilling of the same people: **And when they had prayed, the place was shaken where they were assembled together; and they were all filled with the Holy Ghost, and they spake the word of God with boldness.**

We have already alluded to young Timothy, Paul's son in the faith, who had no doubt been filled with the Spirit through Paul's own ministry. Not many years later (about 14 years, according to Usher's dating)[1] Paul deemed it necessary to urge upon Timothy, **Wherefore I put thee in remembrance that thou stir up the gift of God, which is in thee by the putting on of my hands** (2 Tim. 1:6).

Likewise the great church at Ephesus was plagued with that eternal tendency toward regression. This church had its beginnings in a blaze of glory. Early on, about 12 of its charter members had come into a vital experience with the Holy Spirit at the hands of Paul: **And when Paul had laid his hands on them, the Holy Ghost came on them; and they spake with tongues, and prophesied** (Acts 19:6). This event took place in about 54 A.D. Even so, some ten years later Paul writes to these same believers saying, **And be not drunk with wine, wherein is excess; but be filled** (better translated "be being filled") **with the Spirit** (Eph. 5:18).

Surely this is ample evidence to support the idea that those who have once been filled with the Spirit have a tendency not to remain Spirit-filled. It follows then that when believers allow the rivers of living water to "stagnate," there will be few gifts manifested.

The second gift-limiting problem is a general lack of understanding relating to the Spirit's gifts. Ignorance regarding the gifts will almost always result in one or two different conditions. Either it will lead to extremes — abuses and misuses — or it will discourage and finally eliminate their manifestation altogether. Certainly neither of these alternatives is desirable.

Gifts of the Spirit are most meaningfully manifested in an atmosphere of faith. And faith's greatest stimulants are knowledge and right understanding. Thus an urgency is laid upon the Church to pursue with diligence a Spirit-enlightened understanding of the gifts.

A final area of concern is a discernable neglect of and failure to follow Paul's strong imperatives relating to the gifts. We should take a look at the composite list. It may surprise you as it did me.

1. **But covet earnestly the best gifts...**(1 Cor. 12:31).

2. **Follow after charity, and desire spiritual gifts...** (1 Cor. 14:1).

3. ...(desire) **rather that ye may prophesy** (1 Cor. 14:1).

4. ...**covet to prophesy...**(1 Cor. 14:39).

5. **Wherefore let him that speaketh in an unknown tongue pray that he may interpret** (1 Cor. 14:13).

In his book, *Dynamics of Spiritual Gifts*, William McRae puts forth a valiant effort to discourage personal prayer for gifts of the Spirit. He says: "Gifts are not even distributed on the basis of prayer. Some will object to this statement on the basis of 1 Corinthians 12:31, 'Earnestly desire the greater gifts.' However it ought to be noted that this is second person plural, not singular, imperative in the Greek text. This seems to imply the entire body is being addressed, not individuals in the church."[2]

However, in his effort to discount personal pursuit of spiritual gifts, Mr. McRae overlooks some salient points:

1. The gifts are bestowed upon individuals. Where there is no individual application, corporate pursuit will be fruitless: **Now ye are the body of Christ, and members in particular** (1 Cor. 12:27).

2. The parallel passage, 1 Corinthians 14:1, certainly sets forth the idea of personal pursuit when it instructs, **...desire spiritual gifts, but rather that ye may prophesy.** The inference is unmistakable — "You, as individuals, desire spiritual gifts, but rather that you, as individuals, may prophesy." There is no way the corporate body can prophesy. It is individuals who do it.

3. In 1 Corinthians 14:13, there is a forthright command for individuals to pray for a specific gift: **Wherefore let him that speaketh in an unknown tongue pray that he may interpret.**

Consider now Paul's imperatives.

What a strong imperative is this: "But covet earnestly the best gifts." While the term *covet* usually appears in Scripture in connection with things forbidden, here a form of coveting is strongly urged in regard to spiritual gifts. The word *covet* literally means "to be zealous for" or "to desire strongly." The idea set forth is that we should do whatever is required to obtain that which we desire.

I will illustrate. When I was 16 years old, my family and I attended a farm picnic on a Sunday afternoon. Since most of our family had recently found the Lord and were only beginning to get acquainted with the family of God, the majority of the people gathered there, including a large group of young folks, were strangers to us.

As I mingled with the crowd, I was especially attracted to one of the young ladies. In fact, I guess you could say that it was love at first sight! In spite of my youthfulness, I said in my heart, "That is the girl I want to marry some day."

Sometimes desire and fulfillment are a piece apart. But my heart was fixed. I was willing to pay just about any price to gain my heart's desire. I was to learn that the girl of my dreams had the highest of standards and ideals. She didn't like slang, of which I used a plenty, having so recently turned to the Lord. So I quit my slang — an excellent thing for a Christian to do anyway. Furthermore, she had an aversion to the funny papers, to which I was a devotee. For her sake — and perhaps to my own betterment — I quit them. Anything to please her, that I was ready to do. For you see, I sincerely desired her. But all of my doing didn't seem to avail a great deal. Oh, yes, we were friends. When apart we corresponded, but our letters were anything but romantic. Nevertheless, my desire persisted. Someone once said, "That at which we aim, we usually obtain."

Some years passed and then one day a ray of hope burst on the horizon. I received another of those very casual letters from my beloved, but I could hardly believe my eyes when I saw that it was signed, "With love." Always thereafter, although until then I had never had the courage, I signed my letters, "With love."

At long length my desire paid off. From the birth of the desire until the payoff was 7 years. We have now been married nearly 50 years, and I am still exceedingly grateful that strong desire persisted.

When believers begin to desire spiritual gifts with a similar fervor, a veritable revolution will occur.

Passivity is our problem. Half-heartedness is the curse of the kingdom: **And there is none that calleth upon thy name, that stirreth up himself to take hold of thee...** (Is. 64:7). Yet we have tremendous encouragement from the Lord: **And ye shall seek me, and find me, when ye shall search for me with all your heart** (Jer. 29:13).

The object of our desire is to be "the best gifts." What the best gifts are is not clearly defined, and may not be easily ascertained. If best is to be determined by order of listing, we would have to conclude from the list in 1 Corinthians 12:8-10 that the best gift is "the word of wisdom." From the list in 1 Corinthians 12:28, however, we would understand it to be "apostles." But such a conclusion poses a difficulty, for here Paul mingles ministry gifts of Christ (see Eph. 4:11) with gifts of the Holy Ghost. Again, from Paul's statement in 1 Corinthians 14:1, "but (covet) rather (that is, most of all or more than any other) that ye may prophesy," we have a strong indication that prophecy is the best gift. Add to this the observations in my book, *Charismatics, Are We Missing Something?*, in the chapter entitled "Tongues, the Greatest Gift," and you have a somewhat confused picture.

However, I am persuaded that there is an acceptable solution to the problem. Jesus Himself established a principle relating to greatness which applies beautifully here. Admittedly He was addressing the question of comparative greatness among people, but the same principle certainly applies to gifts of the Spirit. His assertion was, **But he that is greatest among you shall be your servant** (Matt. 23:11). That is to say, the greatest servant is the greatest person. Transferring this principle to the gifts, we then draw this conclusion: the greatest or best gift is that gift which renders the greatest or best service. In that light, the best gift would be determined by the circumstance or situation at hand. For example, after an utterance in tongues has occurred in the congregation, the best gift for that moment would be the interpretation of tongues.

Another imperative appears in 1 Corinthians 14:1: "desire spiritual gifts." The same Greek word translated "covet earnestly" in 1 Corinthians 12:31 is here translated "desire." Thus the double emphasis made by Paul should not be lightly passed over.

Desire is vital. When the importance and meaningfulness of the gifts is not perceived, and when the gifts are looked upon as appendages of little importance, there will be little desire for them. And where sincere desire is lacking, there also the gifts will be wanting.

Another thing, desire does not arise where availability is doubted. Some teach that the Spirit's gifts were only for the Apostolic Age and for the sole purpose of getting the Church launched. The conclusion then is: Why desire what is not available?

Let me give you an example of the kind of teaching to which I allude. William McRae, in his book, *The Dynamics of Spiritual Gifts*,[3] has this to say regarding the various gifts.

1. Gift of the word of wisdom: ". . .we conclude that the gift of wisdom existed only in the first century in the apostolic age, before the completion of the canon of Scripture" (p. 65).

2. Gift of the word of knowledge: "As the New Testament was written and became available, this gift would no longer be necessary" (p. 66.)

3. Gift of faith: (McRae indicates it is for us today. Why only one gift is for us now, while all the others named in 1 Corinthians 12:8-19 are not, creates both hermeneutical and theological problems.)

4. Gifts of healing: "The biblical gift of healing, we believe, was a temporary gift given to confirm the messenger and the message in the days of introducing the new age of Christianity" (p. 72).

5. Gift of miracles: "The nature of the gift and the purpose of the gift suggest it too was a confirmatory gift of the apostolic age" (p. 73).

6. Gift of prophecy: ". . .the gift is no longer present with us, nor has it been present since the days of the early church" (p. 47).

7. Gift of discerning of spirits: "The completion of the canon of Scripture may well have eliminated the need for this gift" (p. 75).

8. Gift of tongues: "The nature and purposes of this gift indicates that it too was a characteristic gift of the apostolic age given to confirm the messenger and his message" (p. 80).

9. Gift of interpretation of tongues: "This accompanied the gift of tongues as a confirmatory gift of the early church" (p. 80).

To hold such views and to propagate them is virtually to quash any interest in the supernatural gifts of the Spirit. We would do well to heed the wise words of British scholar, Harold Horton, when he says: "The loose statements of the commentators on these things have the effect, if not the design of sweeping away the supernatural. Once again it is necessary to warn young Christians against that exegesis that degrades the supernatural in the Bible to the powerless and undistinguished level of the natural."[4]

While we desire to credit McRae and his school of thought with honesty in their view, we believe they are the unwitting victims of human rationalizations akin to that of the religious leaders of Jesus' day.

The argument that the Spirit's gifts were intended only for that period before the canon of Scripture was complete is extremely anemic. By the time 1 Corinthians was written (59 A.D.), the Scriptures wer nearing completion. We wonder why the Holy Spirit would have directed Paul to give so much attention (three whole chapters) to something of such little significance to the ongoing Church.

The further argument that the New Testament itself made the gifts unnecessary is as weak as water. If the manifested Word, Jesus Himself, required confirmatory supernatural manifestations, who is to say that the written Word requires less? Confirmation of the Word is often the crutch which man's faith so badly needs.

Scripture itself does not teach nor even hint that the Spirit's gifts were to be only temporary endowments to get the Church launched. The fact is, it teaches the exact opposite. Of special interest is Paul's comment in 1 Corinthians 13:8-10:

. . . but whether there be prophecies, they shall fail; whether there be tongues, they shall cease; whether there be knowledge, it shall vanish away.

For we know in part, and we prophesy in part.

But when that which is perfect is come, then that which is in part shall be done away.

When Paul speaks of knowledge in verse 8, he is evidently speaking of the word of knowledge. His whole point seems to be that the gifts, which are indeed his subject in this passage, are to be present as long as imperfection prevails. And that will last until imperfection gives way to perfection.

Interestingly, McRae places himself in a rather contradictory stance when he states: "The 'perfect' can hardly be the completion of the canon of Scripture. The coming of the perfect marks the end of the partial. But who would say that we know now as we are known? We still see things vaguely. Many things are still an enigma to us. To say 'the perfect' is the completed New Testament is to claim to see more clearly than Paul and the apostles. Few would make such a claim. The partial knowledge still has not ended. The perfect still has not come. The condition described in verses 10 and 12 will be realized only at the coming of our Lord."[5]

We could not agree more heartily. The gifts are for the now — the entire Church Age. So "follow after charity, and desire spiritual gifts."

The third imperative is attached to the second, and is a sort of qualifier of it. Paul says, "desire spiritual gifts, but rather that ye may prophesy." That is, "in your pursuit of the Spirit's gifts, give prophecy the priority consideration, the reason being that it ranks so high as a force for edificiation." Listen to his rationale:

> But he that prophesieth speaketh unto men to edification, and exhortation, and comfort.
>
> He that speaketh in an unknown tongue edifieth himself; but he that prophesieth edifieth the church.
>
> I would that ye all spake with tongues, but rather that ye prophesied:...that the church may receive edifying....
>
> ...seek that ye may excel to the edifying of the church.
>
> 1 Corinthians 14:3-5,12

The phrase "rather that ye may prophesy" has been commonly employed to give the gift of prophecy degrees of greatness above all other gifts. While that application may have some justification, Paul's intended message seems to be "rather that ye may prophesy than that ye speak with tongues" (it being understood that when tongues are interpreted they are equal to prophecy as a means for edification), for he immediately launches into a comparison of the two gifts — tongues and prophecy — as they relate to force for edification of the Church.

The imperative to prophesy is undergirded with other passages: **For ye may all prophesy...**(1 Cor. 14:31), and **...covet to prophesy...**(1 Cor. 14:39).

A final imperative is seen in 1 Corinthians 14:13: "Wherefore let him that speaketh in an unknown tongue pray that he may interpret." This ought not to be taken lightly, for it places a definite responsibility upon the tongues-speaker in the public service. He is to recognize that the first responsibility for interpretation of his tongues utterance rests squarely upon himself.

We therefore conclude that if the Spirit's gifts are to have their proper place and serve their intended purpose in the Church today, it is our duty and responsibility as believers to pursue with all earnestness the infilling of the Spirit, to diligently seek knowledge and understanding of the Spirit's gifts, and to apply ourselves with determination to the imperatives which Paul has laid upon us.

Notes

[1]*The Scofield Reference Bible* (New York: Oxford University Press, 1909, 1917, 1937, 1945), cf. Usher's dates for Acts 16 and 2 Timothy 1:6, pp. 1171,1279.

[2]William McRae, *Dynamics of Spiritual Gifts* (Grand Rapids: Zondervan Publishing House, 1976), p. 37.

[3]*Ibid.* (see pp. 45,46,64,81).

[4]Harold Horton, *The Gifts of the Spirit*, 10th ed. (Nottingham, England: Assemblies of God Publishing House, 1971), pp. 146,147.

[5]McRae, p. 92.

4
Motivation

Attention was given in the previous chapter to reasons for the scarceness of spiritual gifts today. We cited three in particular:

1. Failure of believers to remain Spirit-filled.
2. Minimal knowledge of the gifts and their functions.
3. Overlooking or neglecting of Paul's imperatives.

Another reason may well be added — lack of proper motivation. What then is proper motivation for spiritual gifts, and why is it important that the gifts be manifested today?

Motivation may come in many forms, some proper and some improper, some profitable and some detrimental. Paul places both the negative and the positive into clear perspective when he says:

> Though I speak with the tongues of men and of angels, and have not charity, I am become as sounding brass, or a tinkling cymbal.
>
> And though I have the gift of prophecy, and understand all mysteries, and all knowledge; and though I have all faith, so that I could remove mountains, and have not charity, I am nothing. . . .
>
> Follow after charity, and desire spiritual gifts. . . .
>
> . . . seek that ye may excel to the edifying of the church.
>
> 1 Corinthians 13:1,2; 14:1,12

Two forms of motivation are in bold relief — self-centered motivation and God-centered motivation, the motive of ulterior purpose and the motive of love. Each form should be examined carefully with the end in mind that we may avoid the type of motivation which brings no glory to God and which hinders rather than furthers the cause of Christ. Rather, let us pursue and espouse that motivation which does glorify God and advance His Kingdom.

Consider the negative form of motivation. What are its identifying marks? Before answering that question, I urge that we use extreme caution in judging the motives of others, remembering that it is only God Who truly sees the heart: **...for man looketh on the outward appearance, but the Lord looketh on the heart** (1 Sam. 16:7). We do much better to discover our own motivation. In so doing, we may ask ourselves two questions: 1) Why do I wish to see the gifts manifested? and, 2) Why do I personally desire to be used in the gifts of the Spirit?

There may be ulterior reasons for wishing to see gifts in operation: Is it possible I have a yen for the spectacular? Is it the excitement generated which intrigues me? Is it that I secretly enjoy being able to boast of the great spirituality of my church as compared to other "dead" churches?

Likewise, there may be ulterior reasons for wishing to be used in manifestation of the gifts of the Spirit: Is it possible my motivation is satisfaction of my own ego and pride? Do I wish to be seen as someone great? Do I desire a basis for boasting?

Let me assure you, these things do occur. A few decades ago, during the period when gifts were supposedly being imparted profusely by certain self-appointed prophets, the wife of a rather prominent pastor, swept off her feet by the tidal wave of evident extremes, was overheard exclaiming about the gifts, "I've got all of them but one!"

There is still another evil which I have witnessed in the areas of motivation. I have seen, on rare occasions, individuals who have sought to impose their own feelings or to gain their own ends through the operation of a gift or gifts. I have heard judgment pronounced through tongues and interpretation, and have witnessed, through the same gifts, attempts to influence important decisions. It is this kind of motivation which brings into disrepute the blessed gifts of the Spirit.

However, ulterior motivation on the part of a few, rather than being permitted to discourage all manifestation of gifts, ought to generate the highest desire in all of us for proper motivation and manifestation.

For this reason 1 Corinthians 13 is exactly where this proper motivation is found, sandwiched in the midst of Paul's discourse on spiritual gifts. His concluding statement in Chapter 12, **...and yet shew I unto you a more excellent way** (v. 31), was not intended to say that love is a "more excellent way" than spiritual gifts, but rather that the gifts operating under love's motivation is the "more excellent way."

There is no higher motivation than love:

Charity (love) **suffereth long, and is kind; charity**

envieth not; charity vaunteth not itself, is not puffed up.

Doth not behave itself unseemly, seeketh not her own, is not easily provoked, thinketh no evil;

Rejoiceth not in iniquity, but rejoiceth in the truth;

Beareth all things, believeth all things, hopeth all things, endureth all things.

Charity never faileth....

1 Corinthians 13:4-8

Our prayer is: "O God, infuse us with these blessed qualities. Overlay us with love's characteristics, as the temple pillars were overlaid with gold, so that the gifts manifested through us may result in the maximum good to the glory of God."

Proper motivation for spiritual gifts interests itself essentially in three directions: 1) Toward God Himself, 2) toward the Body of Christ, and 3) toward the whitened harvest field.

When motivation toward God is correct, all other motivations readily fall in line. This is, at its base, the motivation of love. Love, by its nature, requires full obedience: **If ye love me, keep my commandments** (John 14:15). Jesus is our pattern, His motivation was pure love. Thus He could say of His heavenly Father, **...for I do always those things that please him** (John 8:29). A mind-set to please and honor God then is fundamental to meaningful manifestation of the gifts.

It follows that what springs out of love for God also best serves the Body of Christ. The welfare and blessing of the Body is a chief concern of the Head of the Body, and it must also be the chief concern of the members of the Body. True love will **Let no man seek his own, but every man another's wealth** (1 Cor. 10:24).

Paul's central thrust in 1 Corinthians 14 is the profit and blessing of the Body. It is not difficult to perceive that he is seeking to redirect the Corinthians' motivation away from the "bless-me" syndrome to a "bless-the-Body" motivation. Repeatedly that passion surfaces:

Now, brethren, if I come unto you speaking with tongues, what shall I profit you, except I...(1 Cor. 14:6) **...seek that ye may excel to the edifying of the church** (1 Cor. 14:12). **For thou verily givest thanks well, but the other is not edified** (1 Cor. 14:17). **Yet in the church I had rather speak five words with my understanding, that by my voice I might teach others also, than ten thousand words in an unknown tongue** (1 Cor. 14:19); **...Let all things be done unto edifying** (1 Cor. 14:26); **For ye may all prophesy one by one, that all may learn, and all may be comforted** (1 Cor. 14:31).

In every instance, our attention is directed toward that form of spiritual activity which will accrue to the benefit and blessing of others. And we are reminded once again that love **...seeketh not her own...**(1 Cor. 13:5).

While in Ephesians 4:11-16 Paul is not dealing in particular with the gifts of the Spirit, but rather with ministry gifts bestowed by the ascended Christ, he nonetheless projects the outworking of love's motivation as it relates to the Body. There he says:

But speaking the truth in love, (I pray that you) may grow up unto him in all things, which is the head, even Christ:

> From whom the whole body fitly joined together
> and compacted by that which every joint supplieth,
> according to the effectual working in the measure of
> every part, maketh increase of the body unto the
> edifying of itself in love.

Ephesians 4:15,16

The point is that when each member is motivated by love, he works effectually to the advantage of the whole Body.

While the gifts of the Spirit, motivated by love, are of inestimable value to the Body itself, it is vital that we understand that, also motivated by love, they can be a force for tremendous good in the marketplace. Genuine Christian love reaches ever outward toward the whitened harvest field.

This form of motivation for the gifts is readily seen in the Early Church. Their great and compelling passion was to get the Gospel out to where the need was, as evidenced by their prayer: **...Lord,...grant unto thy servants, that with all boldness they may speak thy word** (Acts 4:29). This noble end then became their motivation to pray for manifestations of the Spirit, which they rightly perceived would enable them to gain the desired objective: **By stretching forth thine hand to heal; and that signs and wonders may be done by the name of thy holy child Jesus** (Acts 4:30). They understood that the manifestations of spiritual gifts and the flashing forth of the supernatural would make them effective in evangelism.

Heaven's motivation both for sending the Holy Spirit and for bestowing the gifts of the Spirit is unmistakably tied to evangelism: **...ye shall receive power, after that the Holy Ghost is come upon you:**

and ye shall be witnesses...(Acts 1:8). Our motivation must be but an extension of heaven's motivation. The gifts were never intended to be an end in themselves, any more than the installing of an engine in an automobile is the ultimate end of the manufacturer. Think again of the ends for which the Spirit's gifts are bestowed upon believers: the exaltation of God, the edification of the Body of Christ, and the evangelization of the lost. These ends then must and will motivate the believer whose highest motivation is love.

5

The Selfsame Spirit

Before proceeding to our study of each of the nine gifts set forth in 1 Corinthians 12:8-10, I want to examine a rather unusual emphasis made by Paul in his introductory remarks in 1 Corinthians 12. You will note, beginning at verse 4 and continuing through verse 11, that Paul employs the expression "the same Spirit" four times, "the same Lord" once, "the same God" once, "the selfsame Spirit" once, and that he infers "the same Spirit" another five times throughout verse 10. Surely this is no literary accident, nor is it intended simply to adorn the dissertation. There is a valid reason for the repetition.

Verse 3 gives us a likely clue as to what this reason is: **Wherefore I give you to understand, that no man speaking by the Spirit of God calleth Jesus accursed: and that no man can say that Jesus is the Lord, but by the Holy Ghost.** *The Zondervan Parallel New Testament in Greek and English* word for word translation of this verse states: **Wherefore I make known to you that no one by (the) Spirit of God speaking says: A Curse (is) Jesus, and no one can say: Lord Jesus, except by (the) Spirit Holy.**

We need to recall who these Corinthians were. Paul says of them, **. . .ye were Gentiles, carried away unto these dumb idols, even as ye were led** (v. 2).

"This characteristic of idols is fixed upon to show that their 'oracles' were mere falsity and pretense. We find an illustration of the epithet in the statue of Isis at Pompeii, where the ruined temple shows the secret stair by which the priest mounted to the back of the statue; and the head of the statue (preserved in the Musco Borbonico) shows the tube which went from the back of the head to the parted lips. Through the tube the priest concealed behind the statue spoke the answers of Isis....The Greek phrase shows that, under the oracular guidance of dumb idols, the Gentiles had been, as it were, drifted hither and thither 'as the winds listed'....Their previous condition of Gentile ignorance rendered it necessary to instruct them fully respecting the nature and discrimination of the charisms of the Spirit."[1]

Our understanding of Paul's whole emphasis will be greatly enhanced if we rightly perceive his intent in using the expression "by the Spirit of God." He is really saying: "...in the Spirit of God; i.e. in the state of spiritual exaltation and ecstasy. The phrase is a Hebrew one to describe inspiration."[2]

But why, we may ask, did Paul consider it necessary to remark on this subject as he did? Why should the Corinthian Christian community need instructions about some kind of an ecstatic utterance in which Jesus was called accursed?

"So terrible an outrage on the conscience of Christians could never have passed unchecked and unpunished, except from the obvious inability of the young community to grapple with the new and perplexing phenomenon of an 'inspiration' which appeared to destroy the personal control of those possessed with it. . . .They would not like to call any one to task for things spoken in a condition which they regarded as wholly supernatural."[3]

What should not happen was happening. There was an intrusion into the Corinthian assembly of a segment of the heathenish or idol-worshipping community. Evidently in the atmosphere charged with the presence of the Holy Spirit, these people gave way to some type of ecstatic utterances which in a way resembled the supernatural glossalalic utterances which flowed from the truly Spirit-filled. This should not be thought too strange, for it was not uncommon for the demon-possessed to cry out loudly when they came into the presence of Jesus during His earthly ministry. Yet the Corinthian church did not understand how to distinguish between that which was a true manifestation of the Spirit and that which flowed from an evil fountain.

To assist them, Paul gave two easily applied tests: 1) If in an ecstatic utterance Jesus was called accursed, they would know with certainty that the one who delivered the message was not speaking in the Holy Spirit; and, 2) if, on the other hand, in an ecstatic utterance the speaker called Jesus "Lord," they would know assuredly that he was speaking by the Spirit of God.

One day while I was ministering in the Yoido Full Gospel Central Church in Seoul, Korea, the world's largest church, there was suddenly a hair-raising cry from a distant balcony. In a moment I noticed several men converge on the person responsible and remove him from the auditorium. After the service had ended, I questioned Pastor Paul Yonggi Cho regarding the strange happening.

"Oh," he said, "that is not uncommon here. The person was cursing Jesus. No doubt our men cast the demon out, and in all likelihood that person will become part of our assembly."

You see, that church understood Paul's guidelines. When they heard the cursing, they knew at once that the person involved was not under the influence of the Holy Spirit, but of some evil spirit, and they acted accordingly.

Another thing of consequence should be noted. There are some who wrongly understand and apply Paul's statement that "...no man can say Jesus is the Lord, but by the Holy Ghost." These people hold that if anyone makes the statement "Jesus is the Lord," he is speaking in the Holy Ghost. That is simply not the case. It is quite possible, for example, to hear those words from a drunkard, a derelict, or an unbeliever. Did not our Lord Himself say, **For many shall come in my name, saying, I am Christ; and shall deceive many** (Matt. 24:5)? This could be translated to state that they **...shall come saying, Christ is Christ....** The point is, people can and will call Jesus "Lord," totally apart from speaking by God's Spirit. Therefore it is imperative that we understand that Paul is addressing himself totally to the matter of ecstatic utterances, and in no sense to ordinary human pronouncements.

Having now delineated the problem present in the Corinthian assembly, we are better able to perceive why Paul gave such strong emphasis to "the same Spirit."

His whole point is that there is but a single Source for the charismata; that is, the Spirit Himself.

Further, it is of no small consequence that Paul so skillfully relates the Spirit's gifts to the triune Godhead. Note his specific reference to each of the three Persons comprising the triune God:

1. The "same Spirit" (v. 4); that is, the Holy Spirit.
2. The "same Lord" (v. 5); that is, the Lord Jesus, the Son.
3. The "same God" (v. 6); that is, God the Father.

While there is a variety of gifts, it is to be understood that there is only one Source, the Holy Spirit: **Now there are diversities of gifts, but the same Spirit** (v. 4).

"Just as the sunlight playing on different surfaces produces a multiplicity of gleams and colours, so the Holy Spirit manifests his presence variously, and even sometimes with sharp contrasts, in different individualities."[4]

And even though the gifts have a common Source, and are manifested according to His determination, the ultimate administration is in "the same Lord" Who is the Head of the Church: **And there are differences of administrations, but the same Lord** (v. 5).

Howbeit, the Spirit and the Son are never divorced from the Father in their activities: **And there are diversities of operations, but it is the same God which worketh all in all** (v. 6).

"God is the Source of all gifts in all men. He is the Sun of the whole universe, and always in the meridian; and from Him as the Father of lights flows every good and perfect gift (James 1:17).''[5] ''...as our Greek Orthodox brethren would be quick to remind us, the ultimate and primary source of the Spirit is not the Son but the Father.''[6]

Therefore though there may be many and divers kind of spirits present in the world, no other spirit, no other being, no other god, can be credited with being the fountainhead for the Spirit's gifts.

There is in this entire section of Scripture an unmistakable inference that the gifts of the Spirit are strictly supernatural in both origin and nature. It is a subtle ploy of the great deceiver to attempt to humanize the supernatural, to reduce the spiritual gifts to the level of mere human endowments, talents, and learned or acquired abilities. When such a view is espoused, the gifts of the Spirit are, for all practical purposes, neutralized.

The word *supernatural* deserves a bit of attention since it has a rather broad definition. Webster says of the word: ''1) of or relating to an order of existence beyond the visible, observable universe; especially of or relating to God or a god, a demigod, spirit, or devil. 2) a: departing from what is usual or normal, especially so as to appear to transcend the laws of nature; b: attributed to an invisible agent (as a ghost or spirit).''[7]

''Supernatural'' can indicate either good or evil forces, and since there is the possible connotation of evil, some become extremely fearful, almost to the point of paranoia, at any employment of the word. This is most unfortunate for a sizable segment of the Christian community, for it sets up a roadblock to their participation in the God-intended manifestations of His Spirit.

Unfortunately, evangelicalism is divided into two distinct camps, not unlike the Sadducees and the Pharisees of Jesus' day: **For the Sadducees say that there is no resurrection, neither angel, nor spirit: but the Pharisees confess both** (Acts 23:8).

While we would not equate any evangelical with the Sadducees, respecting their spiritual state, there is some parallel regarding views of the supernatural. The Sadducees were non-supernaturalists, while the Pharisees freely accepted the idea of the supernatural. In evangelicalism, while one segment, although in no way denying the supernaturalness of God, at least in general practice, denies any place whatever to supernatural manifestations. Another segment fully espouses God's own supernaturalness and in consequence also believes it to be both biblically sound and thoroughly practical to have supernatural manifestations through the Spirit of God. Of course, there are varying degrees of acceptance of both positions.

Harold Horton, the British writer previously referred to, has made some observations and comments regarding the supernatural which are worthy of our thoughtful attention. He says: "...objections to present-day supernatural manifestations are of the class books ...not Scriptural. To ask the objectors to produce chapter and verse is to reduce them to impotence and confusion. And of course, the whole of our attitude to spiritual gifts is determined by our answer to the question, Do you or do you not believe in miracles?

"The man who believes in present-day miracles finds no difficulty in accepting the miracles of the Bible: he spends no time or cunning attempt to account for them on natural grounds. You will never hear one who is familiar with miraculous operations of the Spirit casting doubt upon the Virgin Birth or the divinity of the Lord Jesus.

"How can those who declare that miracles have ceased believe in the imminent and crowning miracle of the coming of the Lord? When the heavens are ablaze with the supernatural splendour of His presence and the saints arise in shining hosts to meet Him, will they stand aloof, incredulous, exclaiming, Impossible! Hysteria! Blasphemous! Satanic!?

"A whole nation missed the miracle of the incarnation through unbelief. Multitudes missed the miracle of the ascension. Will hosts of fearful and incredulous Christians miss the blazing wonder of the Parousia? Can one really believe in a sudden, cataclysmic, multitudinous, magnifical translation of the age-long dead and at the same time doubt and even scorn the sudden and miraculous healing of a fractured rib? Can we really accept without question the cosmic astonishments of Genesis and the supermiraculous re-beginnings of the Revelation, and at the same time reject the miraculous 'commonplaces' of today?"[8]

Many evangelicals who outwardly, and sometimes rather forcefully, discount the present-day supernatural manifestation of gifts are not as opposed to the supernatural as they might appear to be. They believe in prayer, and there is no way to believe in the efficacy of prayer apart from also believing in the supernatural. These same people heartily espouse the idea of the new birth and miraculous coversion, and what is more supernatural than that? They also believe in the supernatural resurrection of Jesus, and they must subscribe to Paul's prayer in Ephesians 1:18-20:

...that ye may know....
...what is the exceeding greatness of his power to us-ward who believe, according to the working of his mighty power,

Which he wrought in Christ, when he raised him from the dead....

We earnestly pray that these friends will dare to reconsider their stance relating to the supernatural, and in so doing will discover exciting and challenging new dimensions to their own experience and ministry.

The modern and vast Charismatic community has subscribed almost totally to the concept of supernatural manifestations. And well it might, for it also perceives that these are the "last days" to which Joel referred when he wrote:

And it shall come to pass in the last days, saith God, I will pour out of my Spirit upon all flesh: and your sons and your daughters shall prophesy, and your young men shall see visions, and your old men shall dream dreams:

And on my servants and on my handmaidens I will pour out in those days of my Spirit; and they shall prophesy.

Acts 2:17,18

Supernatural manifestations and the presence of the Holy Spirit, being witnessed side by side or simultaneously, are more the rule than the exception in both Old and New Testaments.

Believers ought not be obsessed with an unwholesome fear of the supernatural. While admittedly there are unholy forces in the world, God has reassured the believer with a beautiful word:

> **If a son shall ask bread of any of you that is a father, will he give him a stone? or if he ask a fish, will he for a fish give him a serpent?**
>
> **Or if he shall ask an egg, will he offer him a scorpion?**
>
> **If ye then, being evil, know how to give good gifts unto your children: how much more shall your heavenly Father give the Holy Spirit to them that ask him?**
>
> Luke 11:11-13

We do not reject the supernatural manifestation of the gifts of the Holy Spirit because on occasion there may be some unholy manifestation, any more than we reject the idea of there being true believers because there may be an apostate now and then. Furthermore, we ought to remind ourselves that among the nine gifts under consideration there is one gift particularly designed to detect the unholy, the evil, and the false, should it appear — the gift of discerning of spirits.

Once again, I repeat, all nine gifts of 1 Corinthians 12:8-10 are strictly supernatural. They flow forth from the invisible triune God, and in their manifestation they are viewed as "departing from what is usual or normal, especially so as to appear to transcend the laws of nature." They defy human scientific explanation, and are not acquired by ordinary educational processes. No amount of education or learning can produce them. They are not dependent upon innate human qualities.

For example, the word of wisdom might be spoken by a person of even less than ordinary wisdom.

The gifts of the Spirit are not accentuated natural talents and abilities. The least talented or able may as likely be the agent as the most intellectually endowed. They are not the inventions of men, nor are they mere psychological maneuvers or manipulation. They are not limited to the twelve apostles, nor to men only. In the book of Acts there are numerous manifestations of gifts traceable to others than the apostles, including women. To cite a few, we note Stephen (Acts 6:8), Philip (Acts 8:5-7), Ananias (Acts 9:11-17), Agabus (Acts 11:27,28), and the daughters of Philip (Acts 21:8,9). Also the Corinthian church, totally apart from the apostles, was credited with "coming behind in no gift." (1 Cor. 1:7.)

It is my personal conviction that when the Holy Spirit is recognized for Who He truly is, when the gifts are understood for what God intended them to be, and when room and allowance are made for supernatural manifestations in harmony with biblical revelation, the Church will no longer be guilty of **Having a form of godliness, but denying the power thereof**...(2 Tim. 3:5).

Notes

[1]The Very Rev. F. W. Farrar, D.D., *The Pulpit Commentary on 1 Corinthians*, Wartime edition (London and New York: Funk and Wagnalls Company), p. 396.

[2]Ibid.

[3]Ibid., p. 397.

[4]Ibid.

[5]Ibid.

[6]Thomas A. Smail, *The Forgotten Father* (Grand Rapids: William B. Eerdmans Publishing Co., 1980), p. 19.

[7]*Webster's New Collegiate Dictionary* (Springfield, Mass.: G. and C. Merriam Co. Publishers, 1975), p. 1169.

[8]Harold Horton, *The Gifts of the Spirit*, 10th ed. (Nottingham, England: Assemblies of God Publishing House, 1971), p. 37.

Chapter 6
The Word of Wisdom

For to one is given by the Spirit the word of wisdom...

1 Corinthians 12:8

Williamette Christian Center in Eugene, Oregon, was in the midst of a multimillion-dollar building program when a serious financial crunch struck the area. The lumber industry all but collapsed, and many related industries were deeply affected.

As a direct result, the church found itself in extreme financial straits. The staff had to be drastically reduced, and even though stringent steps were taken to cope with the financial pressures, it seemed eventually that there was no way out.

But the pastor believed that God was their Helper. He was deeply assured that God had led them into the building program, and that somehow there was a solution to the overwhelming problem. Accordingly, he made the month of May a season of earnest prayer for the entire church family. On May 29 he sensed the Spirit of God saying to him, "I've taken care of the problem."

Not long afterward, the head of the lending agency, to which the church was in debt for $4,500,000, stated that the church was in the worst financial situation he had ever seen.

Finally, when it seemed there was absolutely no way out, the pastor was advised that he was to have a final meeting to discuss the matter with the head of the lending agency in Portland in three hours. En route he prayed, "It's me again, Lord. What do we do now?" Whereupon he was strangely impressed that he should say to the man, "Is there someone in heaven you want to see besides Jesus?"

"That is a strange thing to say," he thought, "to a man to whom you are indebted for $4,500,000."

For three hours he conversed with the lender in his plush Portland office, but no solution to the problem seemed to surface. The pastor was about to leave but felt that before going he should talk to the man about a personal relationship with the Lord.

"Have you made a decision for Christ?" he queried.

"Yes, I think I have," came a rather cool response.

The pastor reports, "I stood up to leave and the Spirit of God checked me. 'That wasn't what I told you to ask him.' I turned around and said, 'Just a minute, sir; is there somebody in heaven you want to see besides Jesus?' It was like I'd hit him with a club. It was as though I'd struck him with a ball bat. His shoulders started heaving. He just sat down and tears started down his face. So I sat down with him.

"He looked up when he got control and said, 'I'd like to tell you this. All the time you have been talking you have been throwing in these terms, "born from above," "born again." You went over to pay a bill and this man "got saved." Those are terms that my wife used. We are Lutherans. I adored Lydia. Four years ago we got the news that she had cancer. From the time we got the news until she was dead was only four months.

" 'I stood by her casket and I said, "God, You know who I am. You know about this whole thing, but I know I don't have what she had. If it is possible for You to forgive me, I want to be where You are and where she is."

" 'And,' he said, 'I think it happened right there.' "

"It did happen right there," the pastor said. "No doubt about it. That's the kind of God we have. But to make sure, let's pray a prayer for assurance." And the man prayed the sinner's prayer. When they had finished, they were both crying.

As they walked out of the office, the man said, "Reverend, don't worry about that thing. God will help us some way." Now, he had never said that before.

One week before the church's 25th anniversary, the man came to church. He sat down with the pastor and outlined his plans for settling the church's debt:

"This is what we want to do for you. We want to take this first million dollars that you owe, and forgive it. That's a gift. I personally want to give you a quarter of a million dollars to help take care of these needs. We also want to give you another five hundred thousand dollars to pay all your bills, at no interest. We'll tack that on three years from now."

Hearing what had happened, a lady came in and said, "Well, now that I think it's going to go, I'll give you a half a million."

In 15 days the church was completely out of the mess they had been in.

In this enchanting account is a modern-day illustration of the word of wisdom. What had seemed to the pastor to be almost preposterous and bordering on foolishness — to say to a financial tycoon, "Is there someone in heaven you would like to see besides Jesus?" — proved to be the very wisdom of God which produced a solution to an utterly impossible situation.

Upon launching our study of the Spirit's gifts, one by one, I would like for us to remember that our concern is more with seeing *God* in the gifts than with seeing the gifts in *people*. While we certainly do desire to see the gifts manifested through people, we recognize that they will take on whole new dimensions of meaning when they are understood to be unveilings and impartations of God Himself, and in no way the productions of mere human beings.

A case in point is the first gift mentioned: the word of wisdom. How mighty is the impact when people recognize that through the word of wisdom they may be made partakers of a bit of God's infinite wisdom, and be privileged to truly behold a glimpse of His glory.

Consider the profound extent of God's wisdom. There is no better authority than Paul. Through his writings we not only learn of the gift identified as "the word of wisdom," but we are provided some of the most penetrating insights relating to God's great reservoir of wisdom from whence the Holy Spirit draws when He imparts a word of wisdom.

While writing to the Romans, Paul exclaimed, **O the depth of the riches both of the wisdom and knowl-**

edge of God!...(Rom. 11:33). To the Ephesians he spoke of ...**the manifold wisdom of God** (Eph. 3:10), and to the Colossians he announced that in Christ ...**are hid all the treasures of wisdom**...(Col. 2:3). Also, in addressing young Timothy, he soared to the heights of eloquence and revelation when he penned his unforgettable, **Now unto the King eternal, immortal, invisible, the only wise God**...(1 Tim. 1:17).

In the Old Testament, too, God is recogized as the ultimate Source of wisdom. Traced directly to God is the wisdom of the world's wisest man, Solomon:

> **And God said unto him (Solomon), Because thou hast asked this thing, and hast not asked for thyself long life; neither hast asked riches for thyself, nor hast asked the life of thine enemies; but hast asked for thyself understanding to discern judgment;**
>
> **Behold, I have done according to thy words: lo, I have given thee a wise and an understanding heart....**
>
> 1 Kings 3:11,12

Solomon's book of proverbs is replete with the praise of wisdom, and with acknowledgment of God as the Source of wisdom:

> **For the Lord giveth wisdom: out of his mouth cometh knowledge and understanding.**
>
> **He layeth up sound wisdom for the righteous....**
>
> Proverbs 2:6,7

> **Happy is the man that findeth wisdom, and the man that getteth understanding.**
>
> **For the merchandise of it is better than the merchandise of silver, and the gain thereof than fine gold.**

> She is more precious than rubies: and all the things thou canst desire are not to be compared unto her.
>
> Length of days is in her right hand; and in her left hand riches and honour.
>
> Her ways are ways of pleasantness, and all her paths are peace.
>
> She is a tree of life to them that lay hold upon her: and happy is every one that retaineth her.
>
> The Lord by wisdom hath founded the earth; by understanding hath he established the heavens.
>
> Proverbs 3:13-19

Add to all of this Daniel's delightful appraisal, **. . . Blessed be the name of God for ever and ever: for wisdom and might are his** (Dan. 2:20). Surely it becomes crystal clear that the fountainhead of wisdom is God.

Add again wisdom's own testimony:

> The Lord possessed me (wisdom) in the beginning of his way, before his works of old.
>
> I was set up from everlasting, from the beginning, or ever the earth was.
>
> When there were no depths, I was brought forth; when there were no fountains abounding with water.
>
> Before the mountains were settled, before the hills was I brought forth:
>
> While as yet he had not made the earth, nor the fields, nor the highest part of the dust of the world.
>
> When he prepared the heavens, I was there: when he set a compass upon the face of the depth:
>
> When he established the clouds above: when he strengthened the fountains of the deep:

> When he gave to the sea his decree, that the waters should not pass his commandment: when he appointed the foundations of the earth:

> Then I was by him, as one brought up with him: and I was daily his delight, rejoicing always before him.

Proverbs 8:22-30

Set over against this unfathomable and unlimited wisdom of God is man's wholly inadequate and extremely limited supply of wisdom. But man in his blindness, pride and conceit is inclined to count himself so wise that he doesn't need the wisdom of God. Paul laid his finger on reality when, in describing the evolution of the heathen, he said of them, **Professing themselves to be wise, they become fools** (Rom. 1:22).

Writing to the Corinthians, Paul again evaluates man's wisdom and places a low premium on it by saying:

> For it is written, I will destroy the wisdom of the wise, and will bring to nothing the understanding of the prudent.

> Where is the wise? where is the scribe? where is the disputer of this world? hath not God made foolish the wisdom of this world?

1 Corinthians 1:19-20

> Let no man deceive himself. If any man among you seemeth to be wise in this world, let him become a fool, that he may be wise.

> For the wisdom of this world is foolishness with God. For it is written, He taketh the wise in their own craftiness.

> And again, The Lord knoweth the thoughts of the wise, that they are vain.

1 Corinthians 3:18-20

Who then can question man's need for God's wisdom? But how, we may ask, can we tap into that mighty reservoir? Scripture answers that question very forthrightly, as we shall see.

How glorious is the thought that God's wisdom is made available to us poor mortals. And that wisdom is appropriated and experienced in several ways.

Both David and his son, Solomon, understood and declared that **The fear of the Lord is the beginning of wisdom...**(Ps. 111:10; Prov. 9:10). The statement may be understood in two ways, and both are correct. First, when man begins to fear God, he thrusts open the door for wisdom's entry. And, second, wisdom at its commencement in the human heart triggers the fear of God.

Very closely allied to the idea set forth above are Paul's statements, **But unto them which are called, both Jews and Greeks, Christ the power of God, and the wisdom of God** (1 Cor. 1:24), and, **But of him are ye in Christ Jesus, who of God is made unto us wisdom...**(1 Cor. 1:30). Here Christ is identified as the personification of wisdom. He is the wisdom of God functioning at its highest level, bringing about the salvation of man. And in His Church this wisdom is displayed as a spectacle for heavenly principalities and powers to behold: **To the intent that now unto the principalities and powers in heavenly places might be known by the church the manifold wisdom of God** (Eph. 3:10).

Thus we conclude that the divine wisdom is experienced by those who fear God, and by those who, in obeying the Gospel, receive Christ. But that is not all. The divine wisdom is made available to the family of God in a very general and practical way in response to believing prayer: **If any of you lack wisdom, let him ask of God, that giveth to all men liberally, and upbraideth not; and it shall be given him** (James 1:5). While James relates this admonition to the besetting trials of life, God's provision of wisdom in a general sense surely has a broader application.

However, we need to see that all of the applications of divine wisdom which we have already considered do not qualify for or fit the particular category which Paul identified as "the word of wisdom."

Therefore, it is of consequence that we carefully define the word of wisdom.

L. Thomas Holdcroft, in his book *The Holy Spirit*, defines the gift as: ". . .a statement of pronouncement that is prudent, shrewd, and clever. It consists of a capacity at the appropriate time, and on behalf of a particular issue, to exercise superior good judgment. The outcome has the appearance of great skill, wise experience, or even judicious cunning. One who exercises this gift enjoys a specific insight into the mind and purpose of God that can be translated into ordinary problems and issues of life."[1]

Of the word of wisdom, G. Raymond Carlson, General Superintendent of the Assemblies of God, states: "The word of wisdom is not diplomacy, tact, human skill, glorified intelligence, or psychology. No amount of experience develops this wisdom; it is supernatural. It is wisdom given of God through the Holy Spirit for the need of the hour. Jesus spoke of this when He said, *'When they bring you unto the synagogues,* and unto magistrates, and powers, take ye no thought how or what thing ye shall answer, or what ye shall say: For the Holy Ghost shall teach you in the same hour what ye ought to say. . . . For I will give you a mouth and wisdom, which all your adversaries shall not be able to gainsay nor resist' Luke 12:11,12; 21:15."[2]

Of the same gift, Harold Horton states: "The word of wisdom is therefore the supernatural revelation, by the Spirit, of divine purpose; the supernatural declaration of the mind and will of God; the supernatural unfolding of His plans and purposes concerning things, places, people, individuals, communities, nations."[3]

The renowned British scholar, Donald Gee, provides another valuable insight relating to manifestation of the gift. "There is," he explains, "a sense of the divine, a consciousness of an utterance transcending all the stores of human experience. One is deeply conscious that the right thing has been said."[4]

While it is doubtful that a composite of these definitions could be improved upon to any great degree, for the sake of keeping before us a strong emphasis on the gift's source, I am adding my own rather simple definition:

The word of wisdom is a special impartation of a segment of God's own wisdom, by the Holy Spirit, to and/or usually through a member of the Body, in behalf of the Kingdom of God.

It is not without significance that this gift is not called "the gift of wisdom," but rather "the word of wisdom." Solomon, in answer to his unselfish plea was given the gift of wisdom. For him this was a constant and permanent endowment, which enabled him to administer the affairs of Israel at the highest level. But the gift of the word of wisdom, while the source is the same, is an impartation of a bit of God's own wisdom at the specific time and for a specific need.

There is a special significance attached to the word *word* in the phrase "the word of wisdom." It springs from the Greek word *logos*, which essentially means "an utterance" or "an expression of God's own wisdom."

Also implied by the expression is the idea of a small portion. Thus, in the word of wisdom a small portion of God's wisdom is uttered or expressed.

Holdcroft espouses this view when he says: "The fact that it is a 'word of' or 'utterance of' implies that the imparted wisdom is neither exhaustive nor univeral, but that which is directed to a particular time and place. As it were, the word of wisdom operates as a 'flash of inspiration.' "[5]

And R. M. Riggs had a similar concept: "Neither is there a transfer of great reservoirs of wisdom and knowledge, but a 'word' — a revelation, an expression sufficient for the occasion — of the wisdom and knowledge of God."[6]

For the purpose of helping us understand the application of this gift in a very practical way, we will look for illustrations from three sources: 1) the life and ministry of Jesus, 2) the Early Church, and 3) contemporary experience.

We look first to the life and ministry of Jesus. Some may question our resorting to Jesus for illustration of the Spirit's gifts on the grounds that He was more than Spirit-filled man, that He was God's Son and therefore had available to Him resources beyond what are available to us, and that He ministered by a means peculiar to Himself. We do agree with Thomas A. Smail that Jesus was more than a Spirit-filled man. Smail says: "I would want to argue. . .that the category of Spirit-filled man is inadequate to comprehend all that the New Testament wants to say about Jesus and the Spirit. . . .But Jesus is more than Spirit-filled man, because the Spirit-filled man is completely and absolutely the recipient of the Spirit and never the disposer and controller of the Spirit. . . .Jesus is baptizer in the Spirit not simply as Spirit-filled man, for this. . .is one thing that no Spirit-filled man is capable of doing."[7]

Even so, we do subscribe to the idea that Jesus' general earthly ministry was carried on at the level of Spirit-filled man. The Apostle Peter, speaking of Jesus' ministry, said that **. . .God anointed Jesus of Nazareth with the Holy Ghost and with power: who went about doing good, and healing all that were oppressed of the devil; for God was with him** (Acts 10:38).

It is noteworthy that Jesus' ministry was exercised more in the marketplace than in the sanctuary. He constantly moved among the people and ministered to them wherever He found them.

In the course of this ministry, the gifts of the Spirit were frequently manifested. While the first gift in His public ministry seems to have been the word of knowledge (as indicated in John 1:45-50), there is also ample evidence of the word of wisdom flashing forth. I will cite an example which speaks beautifully for itself:

> And the scribes and Pharisees brought unto him a woman taken in adultery; and when they had set her in the midst,
>
> They say unto him, Master, this woman was taken in adultery, in the very act.
>
> Now Moses in the law commanded us, that such should be stoned: but what sayest thou?
>
> This they said, tempting him, that they might have to accuse him. But Jesus stooped down, and with his finger wrote on the ground, as though he heard them not.
>
> So when they continued asking him, he lifted up himself, and said unto them, He that is without sin among you, let him first cast a stone at her.
>
> And again he stooped down, and wrote on the ground.
>
> And they which heard it, being convicted by their own conscience, went out one by one, beginning at the eldest, even unto the last....
>
> John 8:3-9

What a profound word of wisdom: "He that is without sin among you, let him first cast a stone at her." Surely we have here a manifestation of God's own incomparable wisdom.

Again in Jesus' ministry the gift of the word of wisdom is readily seen in His exchange with the rich young ruler: . . .**Yet lackest thou one thing: sell all that thou hast, and distribute unto the poor, and thou shalt have treasure in heaven: and come, follow me** (Luke 18:22). Without doubt, it was the profound wisdom of God that searched out the depths of the young man's heart, and showed him the only way that he, who had money as his god, could truly find God.

For an illustration from the Early Church, we consult the book of Acts. There, as we have already noted, it is quite easy to identify at least 10 or 11 manifestations of the word of wisdom.

Before singling out two of these, it should be understood that there is often a co-mingling of gifts. This will generate no particular problem for us when we keep in mind that all of the gifts flow from the same Source — the infinite God.

Consider Peter's Pentecostal sermon in Acts 2. The entire message is a magnificent illustration of the gift of prophecy. Yet, mingled with the prophetic utterance is a strategic word of wisdom, exemplifying God's own inimitable wisdom. It is found in verse 23 in which Peter says of Jesus: **Him, being delivered by the determinate counsel and foreknowledge of God, ye have taken, and by wicked hands have crucified and slain.** When we recall that these words flowed from the lips of an impetuous, "unlearned and ignorant" fisherman, we can only marvel and give glory to God.

Another example of the word of wisdom in the Early Church is to be seen in the scathing denunciation of the Jewish leaders by the deacon, Stephen, who, as a result of his indictment, was subsequently martyred at their hands:

> **Ye stiffnecked and uncircumcised in heart and ears, ye do always resist the Holy Ghost: as your fathers did, so do ye.**

> **Which of the prophets have not your fathers persecuted? and they have slain them which shewed before of the coming of the Just One; of whom ye have been now the betrayers and murderers:**

Who have received the law by the dispositon of angels, and have not kept it.

Acts 7:51-53

This was more than an angry pronouncement for Stephen's persecutors. It was the wisdom of God against which they had no defense.

Before concluding this chapter, I will illustrate the word of wisdom again as it is manifested on the contemporary scene. (It should be noted here that due to its nature, the word of wisdom may be manifested and yet not be perceived for what it really is.)

While serving as a district superintendent, I was invited to sit with a church board as they considered pastoral candidates for their church. At a point in the discussion we had reached a stalemate regarding a likely candidate. Prolonged deliberation had taken place, and it seemed we were at our wit's end, when suddenly one of the board members spoke a simple word which was like a light in the dark. It was indeed a word of wisdom. Immediately, everyone present was in perfect agreement, and the troublesome matter was settled. The young man under consideration was recommended to the congregation. He was elected and in the course of time had a very fruitful and effective ministry in that church.

Notes

[1]L. Thomas Holdcroft, *The Holy Spirit, A Pentecostal Interpretation* (Springfield, Missouri: Gospel Publishing House, 1962, 1971, 1979), p. 146. Original copyright by Leslie Thomas Holdcroft, assigned to Gospel Publishing House.

[2]G. Raymond Carlson, *Spiritual Dynamics* (Springfield, Missouri: Gospel Publishing House, 1976), p. 101.

[3]Harold Horton, *The Gifts of the Spirit*, 10th ed. (Nottingham, England: Assemblies of God Publishing House, 1971), p. 64.

[4]Donald Gee, *Concerning Spiritual Gifts*, 10th ed. (Nottingham, England: Assemblies of God Publishing House), pp. 106-114.

[5]Holdcroft, p. 146.

[6]Ralph M. Riggs, *The Spirit Himself* (Springfield, Missouri: Gospel Publishing House, 1949), p. 123.

[7]Thomas A. Smail, *The Forgotten Father* (Grand Rapids: William B. Eerdmans Publishing Co., 1980), p. 98.

7

The Word of Knowledge

...to another the word of knowledge by the same
Spirit.

1 Corinthians 12:8

For four and one-half years I had been serving as
pastor of First Assembly of God in Billings, Montana.
The final six months of that period of ministry proved
more distressful than all the years of my previous
pastoral experience combined. I seemed to be in
contention with powers of darkness that were bent on
destroying both me and my ministry, and I could not
understand the inward struggle that burdened me
down day after day.

Finally I felt I had no alternative but to resign and
enter a different type of ministry. Numerous
opportunities presented themselves. Plans were
underway to enter full-time into a traveling, Bible-
teaching, preaching ministry. My wife and I sold some
of our belongings and purchased an automobile which
could pull an RV. Soon we were to place our house on
the market, and we would be on our way.

But before our departure, a missionary was to visit
our church. I went to the office of the *Billings Gazette*
to place an ad for the missionary service, and as I was
returning to my car, a strange and unusual thing
happened. Deep within my spirit I sensed the Holy

Spirit saying to me, "Son, you will be staying in Montana." I thought to myself, "How can that be? My plans are all firmed up for leaving the state."

Returning home, I shared the strange-sounding message with my wife, but she didn't know what to make of it any more than I did.

In a day or two we left for Springfield, Missouri, the national headquarters of the Assemblies of God, where I was scheduled to serve on a committee. We had been there scarcely a day when I received a phone call advising me of the tragic death of Earl W. Goodman, District Superintendent of the Assemblies of God in Montana. He had been in a boating accident and had died of overexertion while attempting to swim to shore.

Since I was Assistant Superintendent, that meant that I was now Superintendent of the Montana District, and would be staying in the state. I filled that post for 13 exciting years.

But what of that strange word which had penetrated my consciousness? From whence did it come? I recognized it to have been what Paul identified as a "word of knowledge" given by the Holy Spirit, which became a confirmation of God's will for my future ministry.

In pursuing our study of this gift, we want to keep in focus that all nine of these gifts are reflections and manifestations of the great God from Whom they derive.

God is the repository of all knowledge. He is omniscient. He knows the end from the beginning, and needs no additions to His storehouse of knowledge. His knowledge is total and complete. There need never be any adjustments, alterations or additions.

A. W. Tozer says: "God knows instantly and effortlessly all matter and all matters, all mind and every mind, all spirit and all spirits, all being and every being, all creaturehood and all creatures, every plurality and all pluralities, all law and every law, all relations, all causes, all thoughts, all mysteries, all enigmas, all feelings, all desire, every unuttered secret, all thrones and dominions, all personalities, all things visible and invisible in heaven and in earth, motion, space, time, life, death, good, evil, heaven, and hell."[1]

While some in recent time have taught a doctrine of limited omniscience, the Scriptures set forth no such representation of God. The very term "limited omniscience" is a contradiction, for how can He Who is all-knowing, Who knows the end from the beginning, be in any way limited in His knowledge?

The Bible is replete with both declaration and illustration of God's omniscience. Listen to the prophet Isaiah:

> **With whom took he counsel, and who instructed him, and taught him in the path of judgment, and taught him knowledge...?**
>
> **Isaiah 40:14**

> **Remember the former things of old: for I am God, and there is none else; I am God, and there is none like me,**
>
> **Declaring the end from the beginning, and from ancient times the things that are not yet done....**
>
> **Isaiah 46:9,10**

And then there is that delightful and thought-provoking 139th Psalm. What a revelation of the expanse of God's knowledge relating to human affairs. Surely it is worthy of our most thoughtful attention:

O Lord, thou hast searched me, and known me.

Thou knowest my downsitting and mine uprising, thou understandest my thought afar off.

Thou compassest my path and my lying down, and art acquainted with all my ways.

For there is not a word in my tongue, but, lo, O Lord, thou knowest it altogether.

Thou hast beset me behind and before, and laid thine hand upon me.

Such knowledge is too wonderful for me; it is high, I cannot attain unto it.

Whither shall I go from thy spirit? or whither shall I flee from thy presence?

If I ascend up into heaven, thou art there: if I make my bed in hell, behold, thou art there.

If I take the wings of the morning, and dwell in the uttermost parts of the sea;

Even there shall thy hand lead me, and thy right hand shall hold me.

If I say, Surely the darkness shall cover me; even the night shall be light about me.

Yea, the darkness hideth not from thee; but the night shineth as the day: the darkness and the light are both alike to thee.

For thou hast possessed my reins: thou has covered me in my mother's womb.

I will praise thee; for I am fearfully and wonderfully made: marvellous are thy works; and that my soul knoweth right well.

> My substance was not hid from thee, when I was made in secret, and curiously wrought in the lowest part of the earth.
>
> Thine eyes did see my substance, yet being unperfect; and in thy book all my members were written, which in continuance were fashioned, when as yet there was none of them.
>
> How precious also are thy thoughts unto me, O God! how great is the sum of them!
>
> Psalm 139:1-17

The New Testament is no less explicit in its assertion of the omniscience of God. Paul capsulized it most succinctly when he wrote of Christ, **In whom are hid all the treasures of . . . knowledge** (Col. 2:3).

It should not be thought, then, a thing incredible for the Holy Spirit to surface a necessary bit of this knowledge in behalf of God's Kingdom in the manifestation of the word of knowledge.

To enhance our understanding we will seek to carefully define the gift.

From G. Raymond Carlson we have this insight: "The word of knowledge is a divine communication by revelation of facts relating to earth which are not known. As important as a knowledge of the Word of God is, this gift is not a knowledge of the Word. That knowledge comes by application to prayerful study. It (the gift of knowledge) is God's wireless (radio), knowledge supernaturally imparted, a manifestation of divine achievement; it neither makes a scholar, nor can it be attained by mental acumen, education, study, or experience."[2]

L. Thomas Holdcroft says: "The gift of the word of knowledge is concerned with the immediate awareness of facts without the aid of the senses. It constitutes a sharing of a fragment of God's omniscience, so that God makes known to humans something He knows but they do not.

"The gift of the word of knowledge may extend from awareness of elemental matters to comprehensive facts that only Diety could make known."[3]

Harold Horton also has a helpful word on this subject. "The word of knowledge," he says, "is the supernatural revelation by the Holy Spirit of certain facts in the mind of God. God keeps ever before Him in the storehouse of His mind all the facts of heaven and earth. He knows every person, place and thing in existence, and He is conscious of them all at the same time. It is not that He merely recalls them: that would be memory. It is that He has them ever before Him: that is knowledge. The word of knowledge is the revelation to man by His Spirit of some detail of that all-knowledge."[4]

To these I add my own definition:

The word of knowledge is a special impartation of a bit of God's own knowledge by the Holy Spirit, to and/or through a believer, in behalf of the Kingdom of God.

Again the word *word* is significant, as with the word of wisdom. As we have seen, its meaning is essentially "utterance" or "expression." Inferred also is the idea of a bit or small segment. Thus we conclude that the word of knowledge is the utterance or expression of a small segment of God's knowledge.

The word of knowledge is extensively evident in the ministry of Jesus. A classic example is found in John 1:45-49 where the remarkable conversion of Nathanael becomes the fruit of the gift's operation.

> Philip findeth Nathanael, and saith unto him, We have found him, of whom Moses in the law, and the prophets, did write, Jesus of Nazareth, the son of Joseph.
>
> And Nathanael said unto him, Can there be any good thing come out of Nazareth? Philip saith unto him, Come and see.
>
> Jesus saw Nathanael coming to him, and saith of him, Behold an Israelite indeed, in whom there is no guile!
>
> Nathanael saith unto him, Whence knowest thou me? Jesus answered and said unto him, Before that Philip called thee, when thou wast under the fig tree, I saw thee.
>
> Nathanael answered and saith unto him, Rabbi, thou art the Son of God; thou art the King of Israel.

Commenting on Jesus' statement, "When thou wast under the fig tree, I saw thee," and beautifully portraying the effective functioning of the word of knowledge, a Church of England author states: "It seems to me that the occasion to which our Lord referred must have been one of extreme spiritual interest and memorableness to Nathanael; some hour had passed of commanding influence upon his mind — one of those periods of visitation from the living God, when lives are recommenced, when an old world passes away and a new one has been made, of which the lips have never spoken, and which are among the deepest secrets of the soul.

"It was the conviction that his secret meditation had been surprised, that the unknown Stranger had fathomed the depths of his consciousness, which wrought and wrung the great confession of which we have here a crisp outline."[5]

Thus we have a notable example of the gift functioning in the ministry of Jesus in the marketplace, and as a most effective key to evangelism.

While the word of knowledge can be readily seen in the ministry of Jesus throughout the Gospels, it seems most evident in John's Gospel. Time will not be taken to examine each instance, but for the sake of establishing an awareness of the gift's constancy in Jesus' ministry, I provide the list below:

1. By the word of knowledge He knew the Samaritan woman's past: **. . . Jesus said unto her, Thou hast well said, I have no husband: For thou hast had five husbands; and he whom thou now hast is not thy husband: in that saidst thou truly** (John 4:17,18).

2. By the word of knowledge He announced a healing afar off: **Jesus saith unto him, Go thy way; thy son liveth. . . . And as he was now going down, his servants met him and told him, saying, Thy son liveth** (John 4:50,51).

3. By the word of knowledge He knew what men spoke in secret: **When Jesus knew in himself that his disciples murmured at it, he said unto them, Doth this offend you?** (John 6:61).

4. By the word of knowledge He perceived Judas' devious character: **Jesus answered them, Have**

not I chosen you twelve, and one of you is a devil? (John 6:70).

5. By the word of knowledge He told of Lazarus' death in a distant city: **These things said he: and after that he saith unto them, Our friend Lazarus sleepeth; but I go, that I may awake him out of sleep....Then said Jesus unto them plainly, Lazarus is dead** (John 11:11,14).

6. By the word of knowledge He announced His impending crucifixion: **Then said Jesus, Let her alone: against the day of my burying hath she kept this (John 12:7). And Jesus answered them, saying, The hour is come, that the Son of man should be glorified** (John 12:23).

7. By the word of knowledge He knew from whence He came and where He was going: **Jesus knowing that the Father had given all things into his hands, and that he was come from God, and went to God** (John 13:3).

8. By the word of knowledge He foresaw His coming betrayal: **When Jesus had thus said, he was troubled in spirit, and testified, and said, Verily, verily, I say unto you, that one of you shall betray me** (John 13:21).

9. By the word of knowledge He announced in advance Peter's denial: **Jesus answered him, Wilt thou lay down thy life for my sake?....The cock shall not crow, till thou hast denied me thrice** (John 13:38).

10. By the word of knowledge He forecast coming persecution for His disciples: **They shall put**

you out of the synagogues: yea, the time cometh, that whosoever killeth you will think that he doeth God service** (John 16:2).

11. By the word of knowledge He told of the scattering of His disciples at the time of His crucifixion: **Behold, the hour cometh, yea, is now come, that ye shall be scattered, every man to his own, and shall leave me alone...**(John 16:32).

12. By the word of knowledge He knew the details of His coming suffering, death, and resurrection: **Jesus therefore, knowing all things that should come upon him, went forth...**(John 18:4).

All of the manifestations of the gift in Jesus' ministry notwithstanding, it is perhaps easier for us to relate to manifestations through lesser men, as is the case in the Early Church, where as many as 18 occurrences of this single gift can be noted. Several of these instances are listed below:

1. By the word of knowledge Peter perceived the collaboration and deception of Ananias and Sapphira: **But Peter said, Ananias, why hath Satan filled thine heart to lie to the Holy Ghost, and to keep back part of the price of the land?** (Acts 5:3). **Then Peter said unto her, How is it that ye have agreed together to tempt the Spirit of the Lord?...**(Acts 5:9).

2. By the word of knowledge the disciple Ananias knew exactly where Saul was, what he was doing, that he had seen a vision, that he was a chosen vessel unto the Lord, and that he

would suffer greatly for the Lord: **And the Lord said unto him, Arise, and go into the street which is called Straight, and inquire in the house of Judas for one called Saul, of Tarsus: for, behold, he prayeth, And hath seen in a vision a man named Ananias coming in, and putting his hand on him, that he might receive his sight. . . . for he is a chosen vessel unto me, to bear my name before the Gentiles, and kings, and the children of Israel: For I will shew him how great things he must suffer for my name's sake** (Acts 9:11,12,15,16).

3. By the word of knowledge Peter knew without error how many men had come from Cornelius, and that he was to go with them for God had sent them: **While Peter thought on the vision the Spirit said unto him, Behold, three men seek thee. Arise therefore, and get thee down, and go with them, doubting nothing: for I have sent them** (Acts 10:19,20).

4. By the word of knowledge Paul predicted blindness for Elymas the sorcerer: **And now, behold, the hand of the Lord is upon thee, and thou shalt be blind, not seeing the sun for a season. And immediately there fell on him a mist and a darkness; and he went about seeking some to lead him by the hand** (Acts 13:11).

5. By the word of knowledge Paul knew that no man would hurt him while he ministered in Corinth, and that there would be many converts in the city: **Then spake the Lord to**

Paul. . ., Be not afraid, but speak, and hold not thy peace: For I am with thee, and no man shall set on thee to hurt thee: for I have much people in this city (Acts 18:9,10).

6. By the word of knowledge Paul knew that he would see Rome: **After these things were ended, Paul purposed in the spirit, when he had passed through Macedonia and Achaia, to go to Jerusalem, saying, After I have been there, I must also see Rome** (Acts 19:21).

7. By the word of knowledge Paul knew that difficult times lay ahead for him: **. . .the Holy Ghost witnesseth in every city, saying that bonds and afflictions abide me** (Acts 20:23).

8. By the word of knowledge Paul knew that he and all the men who were with him in a storm-tossed ship would be spared, that the ship would be lost, and that they would be cast ashore: **. . .for there shall be no loss of any man's life among you, but of the ship. . . .Howbeit we must be cast upon a certain island** (Acts 27:22,26).

Two illustrations drawn from contemporary experience will show the meaningful function of this gift, even in our time.

From Miles Finch, pastor of the New Life Christian Center in Polson, Montana, comes this exciting affidavit: "In February, 1978, the night sky of Polson, Montana, was blazing with the intensely hot fire of a large, local furniture store burning to the foundations. Jerry and Pat Fisher, owners, were horrified to realize that all their records, including their accounts receivable ledger, were going up with the smoke. They represented at least $20,000 of now-undocumented bills.

"At least they thought they had lost them. When they saw the melted-down typewriter, disintegrated calculator and file cabinet and its contents, the pile of ashes representing their work desk, they were afraid. But Helen Rettig, a woman given to much prayer and compassion, came up to Pat the next day at church and said, 'I think there is something in the front of your store that is really important!' She had been given that impression during prayer for the Fishers. Pat discounted the statement so much that she didn't even tell Jerry.

"But an urgency was on Helen, so she called Jerry Sunday afternoon saying the same thing. The next morning, Monday, they sorted through the whole store with the insurance adjusters, not seeing anything. But Jerry had hope, and on Monday afternoon he and a hired man started combing the pile of ashes that had been their oak work desk. There they found it — the ledger with covers gone, burned edges, the first page of the 'A' gone but the rest of it thoroughly soaked but readable after drying. All the other records were destroyed. Only that remained — and the rest were obtainable by other means."

And E. M Clark, past president of North Central Bible College in Minneapolis, Minnesota, shared the following affidavit with me relating to a remarkable word of knowledge:

"In December of 1970 I became president of North Central Bible College. One of our first projects was the erection of a lovely chapel seating 1000, and the remodeling and modernizing of many older rooms.

"Our plan was to build a new administration building, which would include a gym and several classrooms. When most of the funds had been raised for this project, we were confronted with an insurmountable obstacle. The city would not allow us to build without supplying more parking. So, with the permission of the donors, we used available funds for building parking ramps. But I told the college board I just didn't have the courage to start the administration building. Although the building was direly needed, I felt someone besides me would have to do it.

"Then in the late summer of 1978 I was asked to speak at a homecoming for the Assembly of God church in Morris, Illinois. After a beautiful day in the church I had stepped back from the pulpit to return the service to the pastor. But Mrs. Powell, the pastor's wife, stepped to the microphone and said, 'Brother Clark, you have had a dream for North Central Bible College that has not yet been fulfilled. In a few days a key man will come into the college. Through him this building will be erected. Have faith, proceed, and God will bring it to pass.'

"On the following Wednesday, Gunnar Danielson called saying he must see me. When he came he stated that God had been dealing with him about the building, and that He had shown him how to get it done. 'One hundred men,' he said, 'will give $10,000 each, totaling $1,000,000 and that will complete the building. I will raise the funds at my own expense.'

"The next day we had a luncheon with a builder, Dick Vanman, and after Gunnar had explained his plan, Dick said, 'I will give $50,000.' It was only then that I told them about the word of knowledge which was given at Morris, Illinois. And immediately each of them doubled his pledge.

"Gunnar traveled all over the country at his own expense raising close to $1,000,000.

"I asked him when God had begun to deal with him about the building, and he told me it was on Tuesday morning after the Sunday night that the word of knowledge was given."

A final and fascinating illustration of the word of knowledge comes from a missionary to Latin America, Janet Hedman.

"One day in May 1981, during our second term of missionary service in Argentina, I was preparing dinner. School was out that day, so all four of our children were at home, each with several friends.

"At 11:45 a.m. I began to sense an urgent need to get alone and pray. I wasn't sure for whom I should pray, but I was sure I must pray. Every room in the house had people in it, so I dashed to the backyard and into an old toolshed and closed the door.

"There, kneeling on the cold, bare floor, I cried out to God for this urgent need, and my husband Victor came to mind. Did he have a need right then? Or what about Miguel, the national pastor of the church where Victor was preaching? They were in the city of Vicuna Mackenna, 200 miles south of our home in Cordoba.

"Several minutes later the toolshed door opened and our 8-year-old daughter Jacqui peeked and said, 'Mommy, what's wrong? We've been looking all over for you. What are you doing in here?'

" 'Honey, someone needs my prayers. Someone is in danger,' I replied. Jacqui stayed by my side until I felt the burden lift, and then together we went back to finish making our dinner.

"About 3 the next morning, my husband Victor arrived home after his long drive from Vicuna Mackenna. He walked in, flipped on the light, and said, 'Jan, if it hadn't been for divine intervention yesterday, Pastor Miguel, his wife, his two children, and I would all be dead.'

"He began unfolding the story. Sometime before dinner, around 11:30 or 11:45, Miguel's wife has been preparing dinner while Miguel and Victor were visiting. The pastor lives in two rooms adjoining the church.

"A well-dressed man came to the door, and Miguel went with him inside the church to talk. When they were alone, the stranger pointed a gun at Miguel and demanded, 'If you don't tell me where my wife is, I'm going to kill you, your family, and that preacher staying with you.' His wife had gotten saved and started attending church. The man, who had a 5-year prison record, had threatened to kill her, but she somehow escaped to a relative's house in the country.

"Calmly Pastor Miguel said, 'You can put that away.' The man could not seem to grasp what Miguel was saying, so Miguel laid his hand on the stranger's head to pray for him. Violently, demon power threw the man to the floor, and Victor heard the thud and rushed in.

"Immediately Victor and the pastor began to pray as the man lay writhing, blaspheming and screaming. Victor rebuked the Satanic forces governing him and shouted, 'We resist you, devil. You must flee. We take authority over you in the name of Jesus.' He rapidly fired off a series of Scripture verses confirming the believer's authority over Satan.

"Then Victor spoke, 'Now, get out!' The man withered and fell limp on the floor, delivered by the power of God.

"The visitor sat up on a bench, and Pastor Miguel said, 'Do you have something to give us?' The man pulled from his pocket the .32-caliber pistol loaded with five bullets — one for each person present. He handed it to Victor, who unloaded it immediately and threw it out of reach. The man, now delivered from Satan's power and in his right mind, was able to grasp the truths of God's saving plan and accepted Christ as his Saviour.

"After Victor told me about the near-tragedy, I told him about my burden for intercession in the toolshed at that very same time. We rejoiced together at the wonderful way God had spared their lives as a result of prayer."[6]

Notes

[1]A. W. Tozer, *The Knowledge of the Holy* (New York: Harper & Row, 1961), p. 62.

[2]G. Raymond Carlson, *Spiritual Dynamics* (Springfield, Missouri: Gospel Publishing House, 1976), p. 102.

[3]L. Thomas Holdcroft, *The Holy Spirit, A Pentecostal Interpretation* (Springfield, Missouri: Gospel Publishing House, 1962, 1971, 1979), pp. 148,149.

[4]Harold Horton, *The Gifts of the Spirit*, 10th ed. (Nottingham, England: Assemblies of God Publishing House, 1971), p. 46.

[5]The Very Rev. F. W. Farrar, D.D. *The Pulpit Commentary on 1 Corinthians* (London and New York: Funk and Wagnalls Company), p. 397.

[6]Jan Hedman, "I Was Sure I Must Pray," *Mountain Movers* (magazine published by Gospel Publishing House, Springfield, Missouri), May 9, 1984, pp. 8,10.

8

The Gift of Faith

To another faith by the same Spirit....
1 Corinthians 12:9

The October 1969 issue of *Christian Life* magazine carried a most remarkable account of a person's being revived from the dead. According to the story, early one morning Sherwin McCurdy of Dallas, Texas, was waiting outside the Amarillo airport for a taxi. Suddenly a frightened nine-year-old boy came running up to him, pleading for help.

"My daddy's dying!" he gasped.

Following the boy, McCurdy came upon a car in the ditch. The driver, a man in his middle years, was obviously dead. An older son indicated that his father had suffered a heart attack about 45 minutes earlier. The son had administered mouth-to-mouth resuscitation, but in vain. Other family members were in hysteria.

Into Sherwin McCurdy's heart came a gift of faith and an urging by the Holy Spirit to command the spirit of death to depart and the spirit of life to return.

McCurdy obeyed. Then he reached in and laid hands on the dead man. He later stated that it was like touching a piece of melting ice. But as soon as he had laid his hand on the cold forehead (the corpse was already frigid and cyanotic in death), the man instantly returned to life and normalcy. As a result of this marvelous experience, the man and his entire family accepted Christ.

As we begin our consideration of the gift of faith, let us be reminded once again that all nine gifts named in 1 Corinthians 12:8-10 find their single source in God, and that they are therefore reflections and unveilings of His great being.

In ordinary thinking patterns, faith is a thing related to man. We think of great faith and little faith. We think of increasing faith and dead faith. We think of the power of faith, and of the quest for faith. And all the while we are thinking of what a person does or does not do that determines his level of faith. But with the gift to faith, the focus of our attention must be transferred from man to God, Who alone is the possessor of perfect faith.

Already we have understood that God possesses all wisdom and all knowledge, and that these are essential qualities of His being. Let it be added here that He is not wise by trying to be wise. He need make no effort to be wise. He is all-wise because of Who He is, and not because of what He does. The same applies to His omniscience. Knowledge is part of God's nature, an attribute of His being. But what about faith? Is faith inherent in God's nature? Does He make an effort toward having faith?

To answer these questions, we need to remember that faith, unlike wisdom and knowledge, cannot exist by itself. Faith is an attitude, a state of mind, an action predicated upon certain information. It is a by-product of knowledge and totally dependent upon it. The degree of faith's perfection is determined exclusively by the base of knowledge upon which it stands. Therefore it can be rightly concluded that God, Who possesses all knowledge, also has perfect faith.

While it is true that faith must necessarily have an object, as this relates to God, it can be stated that God, Who has full and perfect knowledge of Himself, also has perfect faith in Himself. Thus when, through the Holy Spirit, the gift of faith is bestowed, it is truly God's perfect faith in Himself which becomes the gift of faith to the believer.

The perfection of God's faith is demonstrated in the power of His Word. So perfect is His faith that He needs but speak, and whatever He utters becomes reality. It was to this glorious truth that the author of the book of Hebrews gave testimony when he wrote, **Through** (our) **faith we understand that the worlds were framed by the word of God** (God's faith), **so that things which are seen were not made of things which do appear** (Heb. 11:3). And Peter endorsed the same concept when he said, **But the heavens and the earth, which are now, by the same word are kept in store, reserved unto fire against the day of judgment and perdition of ungodly men** (2 Pet. 3:7).

God's perfect faith, springing from His perfection of knowledge, becomes the great creative force. He needs only to speak, and creation happens. That is faith at its highest level, and it is illustrated so graphically in the Creation account. Note Genesis 1:3: **And God said, Let there be light: and there was light.** Throughout Genesis 1 the record is that "God said...and it was so." Eight times in this passage the expression "And God said" is recorded, and equally as many times the evidence is that what He said came into existence.

It was to this perfect kind of faith that Jesus alluded when He exhorted His disciples, **. . . Have faith in God** (Mark 11:22). Or as C. I. Scofield has it in his marginal reference, "Have the faith of God; i.e. the faith which God gives."

The disciples had witnessed a most remarkable thing. They had heard Jesus merely speak a word to an inarticulate fig tree and only hours later had looked upon it and seen that it had *. . . dried up from the roots* (v. 20). Then followed the Master's lesson on the force of that perfect kind of faith (which wrought in Him): **For verily I say unto you, That whosoever shall say unto this mountain, Be thou removed, and be thou cast into the sea; and shall not doubt in his heart, but shall believe that those things which he saith shall come to pass; he shall have whatsoever he saith** (Mark 11:23).

Unfortunately this passage of Scripture has been misunderstood, abused, and employed as a device for gaining every conceivable end. Additional attention will be given to it later, but for the moment we will continue our effort at understanding God's faith.

There is obviously a correlation between perfect faith and performance of the impossible. We remember Jesus' penetrating and challenging words, **. . . If thou canst believe, all things are possible to him that believeth** (Mark 9:23). In another instance He declared, **. . . for with God all things are possible** (Mark 10:27). And again we note the angel's message to Mary, **For with God nothing shall be impossible** (Luke 1:37).

Perfect faith, then, is the only truly successful contender against the impossible.

By God's perfect faith He created the world from nothing, and filled the heavens with those things that declare His glory. By His perfect faith He paved a pathway on dry ground in the midst of the Red Sea. By His perfect faith He caused a virgin to conceive and bear a Son Who was to become the world's Savior. And by His perfect faith He spoke His incorruptible Word, which lives and abides forever, through human instruments.

Now this is the faith which is made available through the gift of faith. It is purely God's kind of faith.

In our pursuit of understanding, relating to the gift of faith, we immediately confront a question: What is the difference between the gift of faith (1 Cor. 12:9), and the fruit of faith (Gal. 5:22,23)? Or is there really any difference?

First off, let it be understood that faith is faith, wherever it is found, and whatever its source. However, it is clear that there are varying kinds and degrees of faith. There is the God kind of faith, the faith of man, and even the faith of devils: **...the devils also believe, and tremble** (James 2:19). There is weak faith and there is strong faith; there is great faith and there is little faith. And there are discernable differences between the gift of faith and the fruit of faith.

As a gift, faith is instant and passing; as a fruit it is constant and growing: **...your faith groweth exceedingly...**(2 Thess. 1:3). As a gift, faith results from being filled with the Spirit; as fruit it results from walking in the Spirit. As a gift it rises strictly at the

Spirit's volition; as a fruit it is dependent upon man's volition.

The difference between faith as a fruit of the Spirit and faith as a gift of the Spirit is like the difference between an orange attached to and growing on a tree, and an orange in a gift fruit basket. While both the attached orange and the gift orange are the same in essence, once the gift orange is given and consumed, its purpose is fulfilled. It no longer exists.

Therefore it can be said, the faith that grows is the fruit of the Spirit, while the sudden reception of faith is the gift of the Spirit.

As with the previous gifts, definition is exceedingly important and helpful.

Harold Horton defines it thusly: "The gift of faith is a supernatural endowment by the Spirit whereby that which is uttered or desired by man, or spoken by God, shall eventually come to pass. The human or divine miracle-utterance, or miracle-assurance covers blessing or cursing, creation or destruction, removal or alternation. It is different from the gift of miracles and the gifts of healings in that often its operations are not immediately or even generally observable."[1]

Of this gift, G. Raymond Carlson says: "The gift of faith is not saving faith, although that too is a gift of God (Ephesians 2:8). J. Narver Gortner states that the gift of faith is mountain-moving faith (Mark 11:23). This faith is no kin to mortal trust; it is special faith, miraculous faith. This is not the faith by which we live; it comes in the emergency, at the moment of extreme need; it is miraculous assurance."[2]

Anthony D. Palma defines the gift as: ". . .a special, supernatural endowment by the Holy Spirit that enables a person to believe for and to expect an extraordinary demonstration of the power of God. This is undoubtedly what is meant by the statement, '. . .all faith, so that I could move mountains' (1 Corinthians 13:2), for in the same context Paul speaks also of glossalalia and prophecy. The raising of people from the dead, such as Dorcas, undoubtedly was a result of the operation of the gift of faith."[3]

The eminent teacher, Donald Gee, wrote regarding the gift of faith: "The spiritual gift of faith is a special quality of faith, sometimes called by our old theologians the 'faith of miracles.' It would seem to come upon certain of God's servants in times of special crisis or opportunity in such mighty power that they are lifted right out of the realm of even natural and ordinary faith in God — and have a divine certainty put within their souls that triumphs over everything. It is a magnificent gift, and is probably exercised frequently with far-reaching results by some unrecognized children of God."[4]

To these I add my own definition:

The gift of faith is a special impartation of a measure of God's own perfect kind of faith, by the Holy Spirit, to a believer in behalf of the Kingdom of God.

In some ways, illustration is better than definition. While definition establishes perimeters and guidelines, illustration provides practical inspiration. Therefore, in relation to each of the gifts we seek to provide both.

Ilustrations of the gift of faith abound in both the ministry of Jesus and in the ministry of the Early

Church, and, thankfully, they are not absent from the contemporary scene.

Let us begin with the ministry of Jesus. Earlier we noted that God's perfect kind of faith, based upon His perfect knowledge, enabled Him to so speak that whatever He uttered became reality. The gift of faith, this perfect kind of faith, is abundantly evident in Jesus' ministry throughout the Gospels. Consider the following instances:

1. He spoke, and leprosy was cleansed: **And Jesus put forth his hand, and touched him, saying, I will; be thou clean. And immediately his leprosy was cleansed** (Matt. 8:3).

2. He spoke, and the raging sea was calmed: **...Then he arose, and rebuked the winds and the sea; and there was a great calm** (Matt. 8:26).

3. He spoke, and a withered arm was made whole: **Then saith he to the man, Stretch forth thine hand. And he stretched it forth; and it was restored whole, like as the other** (Matt. 12:13).

4. He spoke, and the devils came out: **And Jesus rebuked the devil; and he departed out of him: and the child was cured from that very hour** (Matt. 17:18).

5. He spoke, and a fig tree died: **And when he saw a fig tree in the way, he came to it, and found nothing thereon, but leaves only, and said unto it, Let no fruit grow on thee henceforth for ever. And presently the fig tree withered away** (Matt. 21:19).

6. He spoke, and the deaf heard: **And they bring unto him one that was deaf, and had an impediment in his speech....And...he sighed, and saith unto him, Ephphatha, that is, Be opened. And straightway his ears were opened, and the string of his tongue was loosed, and he spake plain** (Mark 7:32,34,35).

7. He spoke, and fisherman found their nets full: **...he said unto Simon, Launch out into the deep, and let down your nets for a draught....And when they had this done, they inclosed a great multitude of fishes...** (Luke 5:4,6).

8. He spoke, and the dead arose: **And he...took her by the hand, and called, saying, Maid, arise. And her spirit came again, and she arose straightway...** (Luke 8:54,55).

9. He spoke, and the cripple were made whole: **And when Jesus saw her, he called her to him, and said unto her, Woman, thou art loosed from thine infirmity....and immediately she was made straight, and glorified God** (Luke 13:12,13).

Before moving on to the Early Church, we should be alerted to note that few of these manifestations of the gift of faith through Jesus' ministry were in a regular meeting place, but most were in the marketplace.

The same gift of faith is wonderfully exemplified in the Early Church. We have seen that God's perfect kind of faith was demonstrated in His own speaking, and in the outcome of that speaking. Likewise, we have seen that through the gift of faith the man Christ Jesus spoke, and what He spoke occurred. Now we shall see that the same gift of faith was present and manifested in the Early Church, and that it issued in the same kind of speaking with similar unusual results. Consider several instances:

1. Peter spoke, and a man lame from birth was healed: **Then Peter said, Silver and gold have I none; but such as I have give I thee: In the name of Jesus of Nazareth rise up and walk....And he leaping up stood, and walked, and entered with them into the temple, walking, and leaping, and praising God** (Acts 3:6,8).

   There are some remarkable things about this account which are deserving of our attention. It seems entirely possible that Jesus Himself had passed by this lame man during His visits to the temple, for he was ...**laid daily at the gate of the temple**...(Acts 3:2). Further, it is very likely that Peter and John had passed by him many times in their frequent visits to the temple. Yet it appears that, until the particular moment of the man's miraculous healing, neither Jesus nor Peter had attempted to bring healing to him. But then suddenly Peter had the gift of faith, given by the Holy Spirit, according to His own will, and he spoke forth, "Rise up and walk," with the delightful result that the man was totally healed.

   Some may question whether this was not a manifestion of a gift of healing or of the gift of the working of miracles, rather than a manifestation of the gift of faith. Our answer is that here we have the co-mingling of gifts, which was not unusual, and which will not create any great concern over pinpointing gifts if we simply remember that they all flow from the same Source.

2. Peter spoke, and a palsied man was healed: **And Peter said unto him, Aeneas, Jesus Christ maketh thee whole: arise, and make thy bed. And he arose immediately** (Acts 9:34).

3. Peter spoke, and the dead lived: **But Peter. . ., turning him to the body, said, Tabitha, arise. And she opened her eyes: and when she saw Peter, she sat up** (Acts 9:40).

Now let us turn our attention to the gift of faith on the contemporary scene. However, before seeking to illustrate the gift with contemporary experience, thought should be given to a quite prevalent concept which tends to be more harmful than helpful.

The concept is that faith results from speaking. Speaking is set forth as the key to faith, and thus speaking is perceived as some sort of magical, generating, creative force for gaining whatever end may be desired. But Scripture addresses this matter quite clearly. It never indicates that speaking is the way to faith, but it does support the opposite thesis, that faith may result in speaking: **We having the same spirit of faith, according as it is written, I believed, and therefore have I spoken; we also believe, and therefore speak** (2 Cor. 4:13). **For with the heart man believeth unto righteousness; and with the mouth confession is made unto salvation** (Rom. 10:10). The order is: first believe, then confess.

The same idea is set forth in the Mark 11 passage, though it is sometimes overlooked. Look at it carefully: **For verily I say unto you, That whosoever shall say unto this mountain, Be thou removed, and be thou cast into the sea; and shall not doubt in his heart, but shall believe that those things which he saith shall come to pass; he shall have whatsoever he saith** (Mark 11:23). The whole point is, if you have the God kind of faith, you can speak and whatever you say will happen. If you don't have that kind of faith (that is, if you are beset with doubt), you may speak, but the thing you say will not happen. Faith must come first, speaking second. Before Jesus said, "he shall have whatsoever he saith," He said, "Have faith in God." (Vs. 23,22.)

As has already been seen, the God kind of faith is predicated upon the knowledge of God. Or to state it another way, God's perfect faith is based upon His perfect knowledge. Add to this the fact that, merged with His perfect knowledge, even to the degree that it is part of that knowledge, is God's perfect will.

Now this kind of faith operates by love: **...but faith...worketh by love** (Gal. 5:6), and love **...seeketh not her own...**(1 Cor. 13:5). Therefore, to apply "he shall have whatsoever he saith" to every selfish wish and imagination of the human heart is to be found in opposition to the very law of love by which the God kind of faith operates. Whatever kind of faith may operate apart from love, even though it should move a mountain, is not the God kind of faith, and it certainly cannot be the blessed gift of faith which is bestowed by the Spirit.

Illustrations of the gift of faith are not uncommon on the contemporary scene. I share one from my own experience.

While serving as district superintendent, at one juncture a sort of political underground developed which threatened the existing structure, and which also had overtones of serious division. I perceived that my own future ministry might be adversely affected.

But rather than making the matter a public issue, I made it a priority prayer concern. As had been my common practice, I based my prayer upon Philippians 4:6,7:

Be careful for nothing; but in every thing by prayer and supplication with thanksgiving let your requests be made known unto God.

And the peace of God, which passeth all understanding, shall keep your hearts and minds through Christ Jesus.

Day after day I prayed, and repeatedly I quoted that passage — and went on worrying.

As time passed, the problem appeared to worsen, and my distress increased. But I continued praying. Months passed, and there was no apparent relief. My praying seemed all in vain. Nevertheless, I prayed on.

Then one day a wonderful thing happened. The passage which I had quoted to the Lord hundreds of times suddenly became like a living thing. Martin Luther said, "The words of Paul are living things. They have hands and feet." That day I knew it. The words of the text laid hold upon my heart, and I found myself, instead of agonizing under the evident circumstances, completely triumphant in my spirit. The struggle was gone, and in its place was "the peace of God which passeth all understanding."

For six months this sense of divine intervention prevailed in my spirit, even though outward circumstances did not visibly improve. But at the end of that period, as if by a sweep of God's mighty hand, the problem dissolved, like a Montana snow before a chinook, never to raise its head again.

What happened to effect such a meaningful solution to such a disturbing set of circumstances? My only answer is, God gave me, through the Holy Spirit, the gift of faith. It was given in a moment. It held me in perfect confidence until the problem was resolved. And then I needed it no longer. Once it possessed me, I spoke to my mountain, and it moved into the sea!

Notes

[1]Harold Horton, *The Gifts of the Spirit,* 10th ed. (Nottingham, England: Assemblies of God Publishing House, 1971), pp. 130,131.

[2]G. Raymond Carlson, *Spiritual Dynamics* (Springfield, Missouri: Gospel Publishing House, 1976), pp. 103,104.

[3]Anthony D. Palma, *The Spirit-God in Action* (Springfield, Missouri: Gospel Publishing House, 1974), p. 83.

[4]Donald Gee, *Concerning Spiritual Gifts,* 10th ed. (Nottingham, England: Assemblies of God Publishing House), p. 36.

9

Gifts of Healing

...to another the gifts of healing by the same
Spirit.

1 Corinthians 12:9

Willis Smith, a pioneer preacher, was opening a
new church in Sioux City, Iowa, in the mid-thirties. On
a bleak, cold day he was visiting in St. Vincent's
Hospital in that city situated on the banks of the
Missouri River.

In the cancer ward of the hospital lay 20-year-old
Faye Betzer, dying of that dread malady. She weighed
only 60 pounds, and although she was caucasian, her
cancer-ravaged body had turned black. She was in a
coma, gasping desperately for breath, with three days
maximum to live, according to the attending physicians.

Faye was not a Christian. She knew nothing about
God. She had no faith of her own, and now she had
slipped into unconsciousness — a very lost, hopeless
soul.

Willis Smith had been to the hospital to pray for
someone, and on his way out he passed the doorway
leading to the room where Faye lay dying. Looking in
he saw the pathetic creature — dark, shriveled, gasping
— lying like a skeleton upon the bed. He didn't know
who she was, but he entered, laid his hand on the
fevered brow and prayed a simple prayer that the Great
Physician would heal her. Then he left.

Three days later Faye left the hospital, walking on her own two feet, made whole by the power of God. She had received a wonderful gift of healing.

Faye's family did not know who the preacher who had prayed for her was, but upon investigation found him to be Willis Smith. Faye's barber uncle, a resident of Climbing Hill, Iowa, population 123, took his family, along with Faye and her family, to Smith's church. There they heard the Gospel of Jesus Christ and found Him as their Lord and Savior.

At one point during an evangelistic crusade in that new church, there were 75 Betzers in a single service. As a direct result of that manifestation of the gift of healing, today there are Betzers all over the world teaching and preaching the Gospel of Christ. One of them is Dan Betzer, internationally known Revivaltime radio broadcast speaker.

Of the nine gifts toward which we are directing our attention, the gifts of healing are perhaps the most broadly pursued and at the same time the most universally needed. Mankind is afflicted, ill and infirm. How large a segment of the human race might be covered by Isaiah's descriptive lines:

> ...the whole head is sick, and the whole heart faint.

> From the sole of the foot even unto the head there is no soundness in it....
>
> Isaiah 1:5,6

There is scarcely a human who can escape the need for physical healing in one way or another. Therefore we say that the need for the gifts of healing is universal. And we can add that this condition will prevail until man is clothed with immortality:

> For I reckon that the sufferings of this present time are not worthy to be compared with the glory which shall be revealed in us.
>
> For the earnest expectation of the creature waiteth for the manifestation of the sons of God....
>
> Because the creature itself also shall be delivered from the bondage of corruption into the glorious liberty of the children of God.
>
> For we know that the whole creation groaneth and travaileth in pain together until now.
>
> And not only they, but ourselves also, which have the firstfruits of the Spirit, even we ourselves groan within ourselves, waiting for the adoption, to wit, the redemption of our body.
>
> **Romans 8:18,19,21-23**

Howbeit, this is not to say that there is no relief for man's present sorry plight. Nevertheless, before giving attention to God's provision, we are well-advised to consider again man's original condition.

Man has not always been weak and sickly and dying. In fact, original man would not ever have had to die had it not been for the intrusion of sin. In Eden the first pair knew no pain, no crying, no sorrow, and no death — until sin entered, devastating that happy condition.

The rather obvious reason for all of this blessedness was that Adam, and later Eve, bore the image of God Who in Himself is the epitomy of wholeness, unity, harmony, peace and completeness. This is not to say, or in any way infer, that God has a physical form or image. Nevertheless, the perfection of His being, we believe, left its imprint upon all of the original creation. It was then that ...**the morning stars sang together, and all the sons of God shouted for joy...** (Job 38:7). So glorious was the state of all of creation that it is doubtful we can come anywhere near conceiving of it. But we can conclude that the first man had no need of healing, for he was health personified. The very harmony and symphony inherent within the being of God lubricated and controlled every cell and fiber of his body. Not the slightest tension existed. There was no cause for sickness, suffering or death.

But then sin entered. Sin is the reflection of another being whose image is as opposite of God's being as night is of day. His is the image of discord, division, rebellion, disunity, tension and friction. He is the archenemy of all that God is. His goal is to destroy the image of God and to replace it with his own image. He it is of whom the prophet wrote:

> ...**O Lucifer, son of the morning! how art thou cut down to the ground, which didst weaken the nations!...**
>
> ...**Is this the man that made the earth to tremble, that did shake kingdoms;**
>
> **That made the world as a wilderness, and destroyed the cities thereof; that opened not the house of his prisoners?**
>
> **Isaiah 14:12,16,17**

And it is also he of whom Jesus said, **The thief cometh not, but for to steal, and to kill, and to destroy...** (John 10:10).

What a terrible day it was in man's history when in Eden the first Adam drank from Satan's pollution-filled cup. It was not unlike the black day when the last Adam drank from the same cup in another garden. In both instances, the partakers suffered unspeakable marring of the glorious image they bore. The last Adam was **...so marred more than any man, and his form more than the sons of men** (Is. 52:14). And His marring resulted in inevitable death, for **...sin, when it is finished, bringeth forth death** (James 1:15).

For the first Adam it was no different, except that his drinking of the cup was in total disobedience to God; while in the case of the last Adam, his drinking was totally in the will of God. In the case of the first Adam, by his drinking he became a sinner; while the last Adam was **...made...to be sin for us, who knew no sin; that we might be made the righteousness of God in him** (2 Cor. 5:21).

But, as we were saying, in both instances, the partakers suffered the marring of the glorious image they bore. In the first Adam the death principle was loosed, and so **...sin entered into the world, and death by sin...** (Rom. 5:12). Thus the door swung ajar for the entrance of sickness, disease, pain and sorrow, and the virtual destruction of the beautiful harmony and peace of man's original being.

What then is the solution for this problem? The ultimate answer is man's return to the image of God. When this has taken place, **...God shall wipe away all tears from their eyes; and there shall be no more death, neither sorrow, nor crying, neither shall there be any more pain: for the former things are passed away** (Rev. 21:4).

But as long as human beings remain in the flesh, there will be need for healing, and one of the ways for this healing to come about is through the gifts of healing which are wrought by the Holy Spirit.

It is of no small consequence that in the Early Church, the gifts of healing were predominately manifested in the marketplace, and they were administered far more to those outside the body of believers than to those within. Today there is vast, and sometimes purely selfish, concern over such questions as: "Is it God's will for *all* to be healed?" and, "What must *I* do to obtain *my* healing?"

And while the issues involved are debated long and hard, there is an inclination toward failing to look beyond ourselves to a dead and lost world, which, if it should get only a glimpse of our great God through a manifested gift of healing, might turn to Him.

How concerned for themselves were those early Christians who prayed:

> **And now, Lord,...grant unto thy servants, that with all boldness they may speak thy word,**

> **By stretching forth thine hand to heal....**
>
> **Acts 4:29,30**

While there are many ramifications to the subject of divine healing, our central concern in this chapter is with the gifts of healing. Therefore we will now seek to define this gift (or gifts) as precisely as possible.

"These gifts," says Harold Horton, "are for the supernatural healing of diseases and infirmities without natural means of any sort. They are the miraculous manifestation of the Spirit for the banishment of all human ills whether organic, functional or nervous, acute or chronic."[1]

R. M. Riggs defines the gifts of healing (or more accurately, the gifts of healings) as "divine enablements to heal the sick apart from the aid of natural means and human skill."[2]

"In the case of this manifestation of the Holy Spirit," says L. Thomas Holdcroft, "not only does the human channel receive a gift, but also that which the Spirit gives the channel to perform is itself the giving of a gift. The relationship might be paraphrased: 'The human channel receives a package of healing remedies to be shared as gifts with others.' The whole procedure is an instance of divine charismata, and therefore neither the personal merit of the one ministering the gift, nor that of the one receiving the healing portion, is the basis of the bestowment. At both levels, it is, as it were, divine charity rather than human merit or even human faith. The sovereignty of the Spirit is particularly in evidence here, and the ultimate recipient of healing administered through the channel of this gift may be either a believer or an unbeliever as the Spirit wills."[3]

As I have done for the other gifts, I will add my own definition:

Gifts of healing are supernatural impartations of God's healing virtue by the Holy Spirit and through a member of the body, in behalf of the sick and/or afflicted, and ultimately in behalf of the Kingdom of God. Or, to state it in other terms, the gifts of healing are manifestations and applications of God's own harmony and wholeness to man's discordant condition.

L. Thomas Holdcroft has provided some excellent additional insights. He says:

"The implication is that he to whom the manifestation of the Spirit is given, is, in turn, given an assortment of individual healing portions to convey to those who need them. In the words of Purkiser: 'These are specific instances of healing.' Or as Corsie comments: 'Every healing is a special gift. There are no healers.' As a gift of the Spirit, God provides healings to equip the Church and its workers with the credentials to fulfill the Great Commission. Donald Gee wrote of the gift of healing: 'It appears to be a spiritual gift especially connected with the ministry of the evangelist, and granted to those called to fill that office....It often gave the apostles an open door in their evangelistic work; as, for instance, the healing of the father of Publius by Paul (Acts 28:8-10).'"[4]

Before proceeding with our usual pattern of illustration from the ministry of Jesus, from the Early Church, and from the contemporary scene, a further word is in order relating to that great reservoir from whence the gifts of healing flow.

God, addressing Israel through His servant Moses, provided a valuable insight into healing when He said: **...If thou wilt diligently hearken to the voice of the Lord thy God, and wilt do that which is right in his sight, and wilt give ear to his commandments, and keep all his statutes, I will put none of these diseases upon thee, which I have brought upon the Egyptians: for I am the Lord that healeth thee** (Ex. 15:26).

Translating this last phrase from the Hebrew, we have, "I am *Jehovah-rapha.*" That is to say, "I am the Lord your healer," or (at least by inference), "I am the Lord your health." In the case of Israel, there would be no need for healing, for they would have God's health. God's point to His people was (by inference), "If you will relate properly to Me, I Myself will be (as the book of Proverbs puts it) . . . **health to thy navel, and marrow to thy bones**" (Prov. 3:8). God told the children of Israel that He Himself would be their health.

This concept, it seems to me, is important to our understanding of the gifts of healing. For the purpose of our own enlightenment, we might label these gifts "gifts of health," for the healings which occur through the gifts of healing are really the outcome of the applications of *Jehovah-rapha* — (again by inference) the Lord, our health.

Our concern then is that *Jehovah-rapha* will be seen in the healings which take place, instead of the more earthly aspect of that application, or instead of the human instruments involved in it. And this was also the concern of the Early Church.

The ever-present tendency is to see the healed one (the lame man leaping and walking and praising God), and to see the human instruments of the healing (Peter and John), but to completely miss seeing *Jehovah-rapha* (the God Whose own wholeness has been so graciously applied to the infirm):

> And when Peter saw it, he answered unto the people, Ye men of Israel, why marvel ye at this? or why look ye so earnestly on us, as though by our own power or holiness we had made this man to walk?
>
> The God of Abraham, and of Isaac, and of Jacob, the God of our fathers. . . .
>
> . . . hath made this man strong. . . (and) hath given him this perfect soundness in the presence of you all.
>
> Acts 3:12,13,16

From the ministry of Jesus we have a bit of supporting or corroborative evidence, in the account of the healing of the woman with the issue of blood. The afflicted woman had forced her way into the presence of Jesus, and had succeeded in touching Him: **And Jesus, immediately knowing in himself that virtue had gone out of him, turned him about in the press, and said, Who touched my clothes?** (Mark 5:30). Something inherent in the being of God, identified here only as "virtue," had flowed out of Jesus. And as it flowed into that emaciated, afficted body, it drove out all that had burdened it down for so long. Thus it is with the gifts of healing. Through them the "virtue" of God is applied by the Holy Spirit to the area of need.

Of all the gifts so evident in Jesus' ministry, the gifts of healing are by far the most prominent and easily identified. I will list a number of representative instances:

1. He healed leprosy: **And, behold, there came a leper and worshipped him, saying, Lord, if thou wilt thou canst make me clean. And Jesus put forth his hand, and touched him, saying, I will; be thou clean. And immediately his leprosy was cleansed** (Matt. 8:2,3).

2. He healed fever: **And when Jesus was come into Peter's house, he saw his wife's mother laid, and sick of a fever. And he touched her hand, and the fever left her...**(Matt. 8:14,15).

3. He healed all manner of sickness and disease: **And Jesus went about...healing every sickness and every disease among the people** (Matt. 9:35).

4. He healed withered hands: **And, behold, there was a man which had his hand withered.... Then saith he to the man, Stretch forth thine hand. And he stretched it forth; and it was restored whole, like as the other** (Matt. 12:10,13).

5. He healed blind eyes: **And, behold, two blind men sitting by the way side, when they heard that Jesus passed by, cried out, saying, Have mercy on us, O Lord, thou Son of David....So Jesus had compassion on them and touched their eyes: and immediately their eyes received sight...** (Matt. 20:30,34).

6. He healed the deaf and the speech-impaired: **And they bring unto him one that was deaf, and had an impediment in his speech....And looking up to heaven, he sighed, and saith unto him, Ephphatha, that is, Be opened. And straightway his ears were opened, and the string of his tongue was loosed, and he spake plain** (Mark 7:32,34,35).

Again, in the Early Church, there were constant manifestations of the gifts of healing. And these, as in the ministry of Jesus, were most commonly in the marketplace. Note the following examples:

1. The lame were healed: **And a certain man lame from his mother's womb was carried, whom they laid daily at the gate of the temple.... Then Peter said, Silver and gold have I none; but such as I have give I thee: In the name of Jesus Christ of Nazareth rise up and walk.... and immediately his feet and ankle bones received strength** (Acts 3:2,6,7).

2. Sick folks and those vexed with unclean spirits were healed: **There came also a multitude out of the cities round about unto Jerusalem, bringing sick folks, and them which were vexed with unclean spirits: and they were healed every one** (Acts 5:16).

3. The palsied and the lame were healed: **Then Philip went down to the city of Samaria....and many taken with palsies, and that were lame, were healed** (Acts 8:5,7).

4. The sick and diseased were healed: **And God wrought special miracles by the hands of Paul: So that from his body were brought unto the sick hankerchiefs or aprons, and the diseases departed from them, and the evil spirits went out of them** (Acts 19:11,12).

5. Those with fever and other complications were healed: **And it came to pass, that the father of Publius lay sick of a fever and of a bloody flux: to whom Paul entered in, and prayed, and laid his hand on him, and healed him** (Acts 28:8).

Affidavits of healings on the contemporary scene abound. To deny that gifts of healing are manifested at this point in time is to deny a veritable mountain of incontrovertible evidence.

When I was nearing 19 years of age, my only sister was born. I am the eldest in a family of six, and my sister is the youngest.

Several months after my sister's birth, my mother experienced a very severe hemorrhage, whereupon my father took her to our family doctor for examination and diagnosis. The doctor was greatly disturbed by what he found and recommended that mother be taken to the Mayo Clinic in Rochester, Minnesota, for immediate attention.

I will never forget the awful day when Dad stopped to see me in Minneapolis, where I was attending college. He was on his way home after Mother's thorough examination by some of the clinic's finest doctors. They had reported to Dad that Mother had one of the worst types of cancer to afflict human beings. The prognosis was that she had from six months to, at the most, two years to live.

Dad was devastated. I remember him sobbing. His heart was broken. He said, "Bob, if you want to see Mother alive, you had better go to Rochester soon. The worst could happen almost any time."

Mother was given radium treatments and stayed on in Rochester for several weeks. Some of my young college friends and I drove down to see her. While in the room alone with Mother, I had a remarkable experience. Taking her in my arms (she was a tiny woman who never weighed more than 115 pounds), I was suddenly possessed by a travail unlike anything I have ever experienced in all my life. It lasted only a short time, but I have often wondered if the Holy Spirit did not employ that means to bring a gift of healing. Eternity will tell.

At any rate, her strength returned and Mother was able to travel home to Dad and the family.

During the months which followed, Mother was prayed for by scores of people. She testified that she never felt anything unusual happen through all of this.

But she continued to regain her strength and was able to carry out the normal household duties of a farmer's wife.

The doctors at the Mayo Clinic had requested that Dad bring Mother back for examination after the fall harvest. To the best of my knowledge, the same doctors who had made the earlier prognosis on the basis of the evidence at hand also made the new examination. You can imagine the joy of my father and all of the family when the doctors reported that they were unable find even a trace of the cancer.

Some 14 years later, Dad received a letter from the Mayo Clinic requesting a report on the circumstances of Mother's death. He responded: "There are no circumstances of her death. She is still alive!"

Mother lived a full 35 years after the devastating prognosis. Thanks be to God, Who by His Holy Spirit brought to her a blessed gift of healing!

Notes

[1]Harold Horton, *The Gifts of the Spirit*, 10th ed. (Nottingham, England: Assemblies of God Publishing House, 1971), p. 103.

[2]Ralph M. Riggs, *The Spirit Himself* (Springfield, Missouri: Gospel Publishing House, 1949), p. 139.

[3]L. Thomas Holdcroft, *The Holy Spirit, A Pentecostal Experience* (Springfield, Missouri: Gospel Publishing House, 1962, 1971, 1979), pp. 153,154.

10
Working of Miracles

To another the working of miracles....

1 Corinthians 12:10

Morris Plotts is a remarkable man. In Africa he is lovingly known as "Bwana Tembo," which means "Lord Elephant." For years he has labored to bring the Gospel to many of Africa's benighted people, often hazarding his very life in the process. Even now at over 80 years of age, he is still engaged in African missions. In a book entitled *Bwana Tembo*, an account of much of his work in Africa, there is recorded a first-hand illustration of a modern-day miracle in the marketplace, one which opened new doors for the Gospel in that area:

"Ali Wamakoya had already demonstrated his friendship by enabling me to work closely with the tribe. That tie was further strengthened by the miraculous healing of Andenda, an elderly blind man in Mumias.

"Hundreds of people were milling around the marketplace that day. In the center of the market was a large cement platform with a corrugated iron roof to keep off the brutal rays of the equatorial sun. A grizzled, white-haired old man with a blanket around his shoulders, a beggar's bowl and a walking stick in his hands, stood nearby. His eyes were covered by a milky-looking substance.

"While I preached, he continually raised his hand in the air. I didn't know what he wanted, so I just ignored his actions.

"When I finished the message, I asked, 'Who will take Jesus Christ as his Saviour?'

"The old man's hand shot up again.

"This time I responded. My assistant, Terrence Mulema, who had been interpreting, and I jumped down from the platform, fought our way through the milling crowd until we reached the old man. We led him in the sinner's prayer and then I felt impressed to lay hands on his head and pray in the Spirit. His eyes began to flutter as I prayed.

"A few moments later, Terrence and I walked away. Unknown to us, Andenda jumped up shortly afterwards and ran through the marketplace. 'I can see,' he yelled. 'I can see.'

"When word reached me about the beggar's healing, I walked to the chief's compound. His assistant grabbed and kissed my hand when he heard I was the one who had prayed for the blind man.

"Finally I located Ali Wamakoya in a Hindu duka. Dressed in his long white robe and red fez, he sat proudly talking with me.

" 'What do you think of the healing of the blind man?' I asked, wanting to make an impression on him about the power of the Gospel.

"He threw his hands up in the air and shouted, 'Allahu akbar.'

"I knew enough Swahili to realize he had said, 'God is great.' We now had an even wider door open to the Wanga tribe. I knew God could transform the lives of countless people as a result of one genuine miracle such as this."[1]

As we have been saying over and over again, the very image of God is reflected in each of the Spirit's gifts. Certainly the working of miracles is no exception to this rule. How can omnipotence be better demonstrated before earthly men than by manifestations of the miraculous? Out from the vast river of God's omnipotence flows the gift of the working of miracles. A miracle is a display of a mere bit of omnipotence.

Omnipotence is a rather common term for defining and describing the inconceivable magnitude of God's power. It addresses itself to power without definitive dimension. Earthly terms like breadth, and length, and depth, and height cannot encompass or contain it. It is power knowing no measure or limit, defying all attempt at comparison, and finding its most appropriate illustration before the eyes of men in the resurrection of Jesus Christ from the dead. And we must remind ourselves that this glorious omnipotence is inherent in the nature of God. He need make no attempt at having it, nor at retaining it. Nor need we have any concern that He may lose it to some subtle enemy or to some other enterprising god.

"God," says A. W. Tozer, "possesses what no creature can: an incomprehensible plentitude of power, potency that is absolute. This we know by divine revelation, but once known it is recognized as being in full accord with reason. Grant that God is infinite and self-existent and we can see at once that He must be all-powerful as well, and reason kneels to worship before the divine omnipotence."[2]

From its illustrious beginning with the creation account in Genesis to its triumphant conclusion in the Revelation, the Bible unashamedly, and without a hint of apology, proclaims God's omnipotence. And the inspired words from the pen of Isaiah shout aloud, **...Behold your God!** (Is. 40:9).

Our understanding of the working of miracles will be greatly enlarged if we will take Isaiah's injunction seriously, meditating soberly upon the greatness and might of our God. Listen to Isaiah's exaltation of the Almighty:

> **Behold, the Lord God will come with strong hand, and his arm shall rule for him: behold, his reward is with him, and his work before him.**
>
> **He shall feed his flock like a shepherd: he shall gather the lambs with his arm, and carry them in his bosom, and shall gently lead those that are with young.**
>
> **Who hath measured the waters in the hollow of his hand, and meted out heaven with the span, and comprehended the dust of the earth in a measure, and weighed the mountains in scales, and the hills in a balance?**
>
> **Who hath directed the Spirit of the Lord, or being his counsellor hath taught him?**
>
> **With whom took he counsel, and who instructed him, and taught him in the path of judgment, and taught him knowledge, and shewed to him the way of understanding?**
>
> **Behold, the nations are as a drop of a bucket, and are counted as the small dust of the balance: behold, he taketh up the isles as a very little thing....**

All nations before him are as nothing; and they are counted to him less than nothing, and vanity.

To whom then will ye liken God? or what likeness will ye compare unto him?...

It is he that sitteth upon the circle of the earth, and the inhabitants thereof are as grasshoppers; that stretcheth out the heavens as a curtain, and spreadeth them out as a tent to dwell in:

That bringeth the princes to nothing; he maketh the judges of the earth as vanity....

Lift up your eyes on high, and behold who hath created these things, that bringeth out their host by number: he called them all by names by the greatness of his might, for that he is strong in power; not one faileth.

Isaiah 40:10-15,17,18,22,23,26

Beyond this, both the Old and the New Testaments are replete with declarations and illustrations of His might and power. I provide the following passages of Scripture for your meditation and contemplation:

Thy right hand, O Lord, is become glorious in power....

Exodus 15:6

Thine, O Lord, is the greatness, and the power, and the glory, and the victory, and the majesty....

1 Chronicles 29:11

God hath spoken once; twice have I heard this; that power belongeth unto God.

Psalm 62:11

Which by his strength setteth fast the mountains; being girded with power.

Psalm 65:6

God came from Teman, and the Holy One from mount Paran. Selah. His glory covered the heavens, and the earth was full of his praise.

And his brightness was as the light; he had horns coming out of his hand: and there was the hiding of his power.

Habakkuk 3:3,4

But that ye may know that the Son of man hath power on earth to forgive sins, (then saith he to the sick of the palsy,) Arise, take up thy bed, and go into thine house.

And he arose, and departed to his house.

But when the multitudes saw it, they marvelled, and glorified God, which had given such power unto men.

Matthew 9:6-8

...All power is given unto me in heaven and in earth.

Matthew 28:18

...The Holy Ghost shall come upon thee, and the power of the Highest shall overshadow thee: therefore also that holy thing which shall be born of thee shall be called the Son of God.

Luke 1:35

...and the power of the Lord was present to heal them.

Luke 5:17

And they were all amazed at the mighty power of God....

Luke 9:43

...Fear him, which after he hath killed hath power to cast into hell; yea, I say unto you, Fear him.

Luke 12:5

...even his eternal power and Godhead....

Romans 1:20

And what is the exceeding greatness of his power....

> **Which he wrought in Christ, when he raised him
> from the dead, and set him at his own right hand in
> the heavenly places,**
>
> **Far above all principality, and power, and might,
> and dominion....**
>
> **Ephesians 1:19-21**

In the face of this vast scriptural evidence of omnipotence, the miraculous should not be thought a thing incredible. Surely omnipotence in action results in the miraculous. There is total compatability between omnipotence and the miraculous. And it is the record of history that whenever the Omnipotent One is manifested, the miraculous is evident. Thus, when the Holy Spirit draws upon the mighty river of omnipotence, the working of miracles becomes possible. In the working of miracles, the Omnipotent One is there for human beings to behold, and thus their faith may be turned from the wisdom of men to the power of God.

Again, definition will enlarge our understanding. Harold Horton says: "A miracle, therefore, is a supernatural intervention in the ordinary course of nature; a temporary suspension of the accustomed order; an interruption of the system of nature as we know it. The gift of the working of miracles operates by the energy or dynamic force of the Spirit in reversals or suspensions of natural laws. A miracle is a sovereign act of the Spirit of God irrespective of laws or systems. A miracle does not, as some cynical unbelievers say, demand the existence of an undiscovered law to explain it. A miracle has no explanation other than the sovereign power of the Lord...."[3]

L. Thomas Holdcroft writes of the word miracle: "...it describes works of supernatural power or deeds of might, rather than marvels or signs. Nevertheless, a miracle often is a sign, for it is an instance when God's working becomes conspicuously recognizable."[4]

According to G. Raymond Carlson: ". . .a miracle is an event in the physical world which cannot be accounted for by any of its known sources. Miracles are works contrary to nature resulting from supernatural intervention, an interruption of the system of nature as we know it. A miracle is a manifestation of supernatural power in the natural realm."[5]

And Anthony D. Palma, speaking of the gift of miracles says: "Literally — workings of miracles. Again, there is diversity within this one gift of the Spirit. It can be distinguished from the gifts of healings in that it includes unusual supernatural demonstrations of God's power apart from those normally associated with healing. Some would include in this the raising of the dead. Sometimes these miracles are the reverse of healings."[6]

My own definition is:

The gift of the working of miracles is a supernatural impartation of a bit of God's omnipotence by the Holy Spirit through a member of the body whereby the humanly impossible is performed in behalf of the Kingdom of God.

Once again we will view this gift as we have the other gifts of the Spirit: first, in the ministry of Jesus; second, in the Early Church; and, finally, as it appears on the contemporary scene.

There is profuse evidence of the gift of the working of miracles in Jesus' ministry. While the list below is not exhaustive, it does bring into focus the commonality of the gift in His short span of public ministry:

1. The miracle of the quieting of the raging sea: **...Then he arose, and rebuked the winds and the sea; and there was a great calm** (Matt. 8:26).

2. The miracle of walking on water: **And in the fourth watch of the night Jesus went unto them, walking on the sea** (Matt. 14:25).

3. The miracle of the coin in the fish's mouth: **Notwithstanding, lest we should offend them, go thou to the sea, and cast an hook, and take up the fish that first cometh up; and when thou hast opened his mouth, thou shalt find a piece of money: that take, and give unto them for me and thee** (Matt. 17:27).

4. The miracle of the remarkable catch of fish: **Now when he had left speaking, he said unto Simon, Launch out into the deep, and let down your nets for a draught. And Simon answering said unto him, Master, we have toiled all the night, and have taken nothing: nevertheless at thy word I will let down the net. And when they had this done, they inclosed a great multitude of fishes: and their net brake** (Luke 5:4-6).

5. The miracle of water turned to wine: **When the ruler of the feast had tasted the water that was made wine, and knew not whence it was: (but the servants which drew the water knew;) the governor of the feast called the bridegroom, And saith unto him, Every man at the beginning doth set forth good wine; and when men have well drunk, then that which is worse: but thou hast kept the good wine until**

now. **This beginning of miracles did Jesus in Cana of Galilee, and manifested forth his glory...**(John 2:9-11).

6. The miracle of raising Lazarus from the dead: **And when he had thus spoken, he cried with a loud voice, Lazarus, come forth. And he that was dead came forth...**(John 11:43,44).

Before seeking to discover the gift of the working of miracles in the Early Church, we should pause for a moment to consider a statement made by Jesus during His own earthly ministry: **Verily, verily, I say unto you, He that believeth on me, the works that I do shall he do also; and greater works than these shall he do; because I go unto my Father** (John 14:12).

Various attempts have been made at explaining, or explaining away, what Jesus said here. Some have set forth the idea that Jesus was speaking of the works of the corporate body of believers when He said "greater works than these shall he do." But Jesus' employment of the singular pronoun "he" three times in this text hardly allows for such an interpretation. We very possibly do most justice to the text when we take it at face value.

It appears that Jesus placed before His followers (us included) a possibility almost beyond human comprehension — greater works than He did. But in order to understand this possibility, it will help to note the prerequisites stated by Jesus.

On the part of His followers the prerequisite is singular and positive — "he that *believeth*." The inference seems to be not only "he that believeth in Me (Jesus)," but "he that believeth for the greater works than these" (that is, "he who believes *for* the miraculous"). Where there is no believing, there will be no seeing; but let the necessary believing occur, and the power for the miraculous is as great as God Himself.

The second prerequisite is of even greater significance than the first, and certainly bears upon it — "because I go unto the Father." Without a doubt we have here a positive reference to the coming of the Holy Spirit through Whose gifts these works would be possible.

Therefore, in the Early Church we have at least a glimpse of what Jesus meant, and we may also have a shadow of what may indeed occur before He returns.

In the book of Acts are recorded numerous manifestations of the gift of working of miracles. Several instances are listed below:

1. A miracle of healing: **And beholding the man which was healed standing with them** (Peter and John), **they** (the Jewish religious leaders) **could say nothing against it. But when they had commanded them to go aside out of the council, they conferred among themselves, Saying, What shall we do to these men? for that indeed a notable miracle hath been done by them is manifest to all them that dwell in Jerusalem; and we cannot deny it** (Acts 4:14-16).

2. The miracle of opened prison doors: **Then the high priest rose up, and all they that were with him...and were filled with indignation, And laid their hands on the apostles, and put them in the common prison. But the angel of the**

Lord by night opened the prison doors, and brought them forth (Acts 5:17-19).

3. The miracle of raising the dead: **But Peter put them all forth, and kneeled down, and prayed; and turning him to the body said, Tabitha, arise. And she opened her eyes: and when she saw Peter, she sat up** (Acts 9:40).

4. A miracle of blindness: **Then Saul, (who also is called Paul,) filled with the Holy Ghost, set his eyes on him, And said....behold, the hand of the Lord is upon thee, and thou shalt be blind, not seeing the sun for a season. And immediately there fell on him a mist and a darkness; and he went about seeking some to lead him by the hand** (Acts 13:9-11).

5. Special miracles of healing: **And God wrought special miracles by the hands of Paul: So that from his body were brought unto the sick handkerchiefs or aprons, and the diseases departed from them, and the evil spirits went out of them** (Acts 19:11,12).

6. The miracle of surviving a snake bite: **And when Paul had gathered a bundle of sticks, and laid them on the fire, there came a viper out of the heat, and fastened on his hand.... And he shook off the beast into the fire, and felt no harm** (Acts 28:3,5).

Murray McLees was preaching in a soccer stadium in Sri Lanka. Suddenly the Spirit of God came upon him and he shocked himself by announcing, "There are two men here who are blind in their left eyes. Please come forward because God wants to heal you."

Numbers of people moved toward the platform, but among them were two men, each of whom was blind in his left eye.

When the first man came, McLees testifies, in his heart he knew for certain that God was going to heal the fellow. McLees prayed for him, and immediately the man could see out of his formerly blind eye.

But when the second man came, it was a different story. As McLees peered into the man's face, he saw only an empty, irritated red eye socket, with no eyeball. Turning to the leader of the meeting, a man named Colton, he said: "This is not the man. He does not have an eyeball!" To which Colton responded, "I'd say he is blind in his left eye!"

McLees said, "Colton, why don't you pray?"

"No," he answered, "you pray, and I will test."

Placing his hand over the empty eye socket, and feeling utterly cold and helpless, McLees cried out, "O God, hear this prayer." Then removing his hand, he saw the man standing there with an eyeball in the left socket, just like the other one, looking back at him — an amazing miracle indeed.

What was the result?

The next night, instead of only hundreds being at the meeting, many thousands jammed the stadium to witness and experience God's mighty works.

Upon returning to the States, McLees shared this seemingly incredible happening with his congregation, whereupon one man in the meeting thought this was too "far out" for him to believe, and decided to begin attending another church.

This man later went to Madras, India, and while walking down the street of that huge Asian city with its teeming millions of people, by the providence of God, met a small-of-stature, dark-complected Indian man who spoke to him in English.

"By the color of your skin and your style of dress, you must be a European or an American," observed the diminutive Oriental.

"Yes," the man replied, "I am an American."

Then began a most remarkable conversation. It turned out that the small dark man was a Christian from Sri Lanka who had been present in the soccer stadium for the very meeting which McLees had preached. Now he was in Madras on vacation. Not only had he witnessed the miracle, but he lived next door to the man whose missing eye had been so marvelously restored.

The Indian told how the man's left eye had been gouged in a fight some 15 years earlier, and that because the wound had become so badly infected, the eyeball had been removed.

"The fellow," the Asian said, "went to the meeting in the soccer stadium, and came home with a new eyeball. He went around the neighborhood saying, 'Look at the new eye I've got. Jesus gave it to me last night.' "

Needless to say, the American was convinced.

That miracle drew the crowds, and, as a result, multitudes heard and responded to the Gospel message.

Notes

[1]Morris Plotts, *Bwana Tembo* (Baton Rouge, Louisiana: Jimmy Swaggart Evangelistic Assn., 1980), pp. 34-36. Used by permission.

[2]A. W. Tozer, *The Knowledge of the Holy* (New York: Harper & Row, 1961), p. 71.

[3]Harold Horton, *The Gifts of the Spirit*, 10th ed. (Nottingham, England: Assemblies of God Publishing House, 1971), p. 118.

[4]L. Thomas Holdcroft, *The Holy Spirit, A Pentecostal Interpretation* (Springfield, Missouri: Gospel Publishing House, 1962, 1971, 1979), p. 158.

[5]G. Raymond Carlson, *Spiritual Dynamics* (Springfield, Missouri: Gospel Publishing House, 1976), p. 105.

[6]Anthony D. Palma, *The Spirit-God in Action* (Springfield, Missouri: Gospel Publishing House, 1974), p. 84.

11
Prophecy

...to another prophecy....

1 Corinthians 12:10

In his book, *Spiritual Gifts*, Donald Gee presents an account which may aid us in our study of the gift of prophecy. Here are his own words:

"Some ten years ago I heard the late W. E. Sangster preach a great sermon in Westminster Central Hall in which he listed ten of the besetting sins and spiritual needs of the British people. I felt quite a special power in his message, but I confess I was surprised to find the next morning that it had hit the headlines of the national dailies. I am sure that Sangster knew something of the unction of the Spirit, and I am sure the Lord spoke by him that historic night. The condemnation of his hearers was all the greater. Messages of that order are far above the little condemnatory messages of lesser men worked up for cheap sensational purposes. There was something sublime about Sangster that night."[1]

In the early 1940s, while I was serving my first pastorate, a pastor friend and I decided to exchange a series of evangelistic meetings with each other. He came to my church for a week, and then I went to his church for a similar period.

During my stay with him, I gave myself extensively to prayer and preparation. Often the entire forenoon was spent in intense application so that I could enter the pulpit with a measure of confidence.

On a certain day I prepared very thoroughly. My outline for the message was complete and I had earnestly sought God. Nevertheless, about the time of the evening meal, an unusual uneasiness seemed to settle upon me. It was impressed upon my spirit that my prepared sermon was not the message for the hour. And the nearer we came to service time, the more I was convinced of this fact.

"But what do I do now?" I mused. I was treading a new path, and, I must confess, I came uncomfortably close to panic.

Finally, I was seated on the platform. The service was under way, and I was "high and dry." Yet in the midst of my perplexity a passage of Scripture began to bear down upon me. I had never to my knowledge preached on that text. But it was all I had. Everything else seemed utterly empty and meaningless for that moment.

When it was time to preach, I stepped to the pulpit, read that text, and from that moment I was carried along as if by a holy wind. Never in my life had I spoken in that manner.

No altar call was needed that night. No one needed to plead for people to seek God. I believe the entire congregation, to the last person, fell to its knees and cried out mightily to God.

Through the ensuing years, as I have pondered that glorious experience, I have been persuaded that that night I experienced the gift of prophecy in its God-intended fashion. And I have coveted it, not only for myself, but for the entire Church.

In our study of each of the Spirit's gifts, to this point, we have seen how dramatically God is revealed in them. It should be noted here that if we desire to better understand the functioning of the gifts of the Spirit, we do well to seek a greater knowledge of God; and likewise, if we desire a better understanding of God, we do well to look closely at the gifts of the Spirit. Each provides understanding and casts light upon the other.

This is true of the gift of prophecy, as we shall now see.

God is very meaningfully seen in the gift of prophecy, for He is, by His very nature, prophetic. By applying the term "prophetic" to God, I mean that He speaks forth; He speaks with utmost authority; He speaks to convey life; He speaks to edify, exhort and comfort; He speaks with the future in focus, as if it were the present.

The Bible itself testifies to the God Who speaks forth:

> **God, who at sundry times and in divers manners spake in time past unto the fathers by the prophets,**
>
> **Hath in these last days spoken unto us by his Son....**
>
> **Hebrews 1:1,2**

In the Greek, two words profoundly disclose the uttering-forth aspect of God's nature: 1) *logos* and

2) *rhema. According to Strong, logos* means "something *said*," particularly "the Divine *Expression*"[2]*; and rhema* means "an *utterance.*"[3] While both words are employed somewhat interchangeably in Scripture, *rhema* does seem to convey the utterance aspect of God's nature.

An example of this utterance aspect, characteristic of God, is seen in the words of the psalmist:

> The voice of the Lord is upon the waters: the God of glory thundereth: the Lord is upon many waters.
>
> The voice of the Lord is powerful; the voice of the Lord is full of majesty.
>
> The voice of the Lord breaketh the cedars; yea, the Lord breaketh the cedars of Lebanon....
>
> The voice of the Lord divideth the flames of fire.
>
> The voice of the Lord shaketh the wilderness....
>
> The voice of the Lord maketh the hinds to calve, and discovereth the forests....
>
> **Psalm 29:3-5,7-9**

Then, too, God speaks forth with utmost authority. No word of His falls to the ground. He declares: **So shall my word be that goeth forth out of my mouth: it shall not return unto me void, but it shall accomplish that which I please, and it shall prosper in the thing whereto I sent it** (Is. 55:11). **The word of God is living and active. Sharper than any double-edged sword, it penetrates even to dividing soul and spirit, joints and marrow; it judges the thoughts and attitudes of the heart** (Heb. 4:12 NIV).

Life itself is conveyed when God utters forth His Word. Jesus stated it so clearly: **...the words that I speak unto you, they are spirit, and they are life** (John 6:63). Herein is to be seen, as if under a floodlight, God's prophetic nature.

The word *spirit* springs from a root word essentially meaning "breath." Thus we understand that Jesus was saying that the words He uttered — God's words — were freighted with the breath of life; they were a life-giving force wherever they were received.

Further, God's prophetic nature looms into focus when attention is directed to the edifying, exhorting and comforting aspects of His utterance. To these ends, it can be said, the majority of His utterance is directed.

A final aspect of God's prophetic nature is evidenced in His pronouncements relating to the future as though it were present or already history. Prophecy relating to the future is purely and simply a reflection of God's omniscience.

Taking together all of these impressive aspects of God's prophetic nature, we have a delightful revelation of one facet of His magnificent being.

Related to our discussion of God's prophetic nature is the fact that even from antiquity, when His Spirit fell upon people they quite commonly burst forth in prophetic utterance. A classic example is recorded in Numbers 11:24-29:

> And Moses went out, and told the people the words of the Lord, and gathered the seventy men of the elders of the people, and set them round about the tabernacle.
>
> And the Lord came down in a cloud, and spake unto him, and took of the spirit that was upon him, and gave it unto the seventy elders: and it came to pass, that, when the spirit rested upon them, they prophesied, and did not cease.
>
> But there remained two of the men in the camp, the name of the one was Eldad, and the name of the

> other Medad: and the spirit rested upon them; and they were of them that were written, but went not out unto the tabernacle: and they prophesied in the camp.
>
> And there ran a young man, and told Moses, and said, Eldad and Medad do prophesy in the camp.
>
> And Joshua the son of Nun, the servant of Moses, one of his young men, answered and said, My lord Moses, forbid them.
>
> And Moses said unto him, . . .would God that all the Lord's people were prophets, and that the Lord would put his spirit upon them!

God's own prophetic nature found expression through people upon whom His Spirit rested. The Holy Spirit Who fell upon men, as could be expected, caused them to act in harmony with God's own nature.

Some interesting lines in the account of Samuel's anointing of Saul to become king of Israel further underscore the idea:

> And the Spirit of the Lord will come upon thee, and thou shalt prophesy. . . .
>
> And when they came thither to the hill, behold, a company of prophets met him; and the Spirit of God came upon him, and he prophesied among them.
>
> 1 Samuel 10:6,10

Now it is out of this prophetic nature, which is an integral part of God's being, that the Holy Spirit bestows the gift of prophecy. As we have already seen, the gift of prophecy encompasses a rather broad spectrum of manifestation. This, as we shall now note, is further supported by a variety of definitions of the gifts.

We resort first to Harold Horton, who in his inimitable style, says of prophecy:

"To 'flow forth' is the lovely meaning of the commonest Hebrew word, Naba! To 'bubble forth, like a fountain' says one. As the heart of the Psalmist when it was bubbling up or boiling over with a good matter touching the King! Hallelujah! 'To let drop' is the meaning of another delightful Hebrew word: to let drop like golden oil in ripened olive yards; or honey from the crammed honeycomb; or sprinkling rain from the bursting clouds. And the meaning of yet another Hebrew word is 'to lift up' — like coloured banners with mystic devices, or silver clarions with flourishes of solemnity or delight. To flow forth — tumble forth — spring forth! You that prophesy! — do not these Hebrew words exactly describe your precious fountain? Who would not covet thus to prophesy?"[4]

From Dennis Bennett we have this insight: "The gift of prophecy is manifested when believers speak the mind of God, by the inspiration of the Holy Spirit, and not from their own thoughts. It is supernatural speech in a known language. Prophecy is not a 'private' gift, but is always brought to a group of believers, although it may be for one or more individuals who are present."[5]

Donald Gee is very helpful on this subject. From his fountain of wisdom comes this observation: "It is impossible to separate true prophesying from the idea of definite inspiration. 'The prophet spoke more from the impulse of sudden revelation of the moment ("apokalupsis" — 1 Cor. 14:30). . . .The idea of speaking from an immediate revelation seems here to be fundamental, as relating either to future events, or to the mind of the Spirit in general' (Robinson Lex., p. 693)."[6]

L. Thomas Holdcroft provides some additional light. "The gift of prophecy," he says, "provides a message from God through a human channel. In many instances, prophecy has much in common with anointed preaching, and in their effect upon an audience, the two procedures could be indistinguishable. However, prophecy does not involve specific preparation by study and research, evaluation of what should be said, or the preparation of outline notes. The basis of prophecy is a personal revelation of the mind and will of God by direct impression." [7]

To these I add my own definition:

The gift of prophecy is a supernatural utterance springing out of God's own prophetic nature, and brought about by the Holy Spirit through a believer, whereby he (the believer) is enabled to speak forth with an authority not his own, unto the edification, exhortation or comfort of other believers, or to the conviction and salvation of the unbeliever.

We must differentiate between the gift of prophecy and the gift of prophets. In 1 Corinthians 12:8-10, Paul states, **For to one is given by the Spirit the word of wisdom....to another prophecy.... Then in Ephesians 4:11, he says of Christ, And he gave some, apostles; and some, prophets....** Thus prophecy is a gift of the Spirit to the Body, while the prophet is Christ's gift to the Church. Prophecy is a function, a manner of speaking; while the prophet is an officer, a spiritual leader.

It should also be noted that Paul, when speaking of the gift, said, **For ye may all prophesy...**(1 Cor. 14:31). The key word is "all," which opens the door to every member of the Body to participate. But when speaking in regard to the office of the prophet, Paul said that Christ "gave some. . .prophets," indicating that the office was for only a limited number within the Body.

Consider now the purposes for the gift of prophecy. It should be understood at the outset that prophecy is not generally given for personal guidance. Abuses and/or misuses of any gift create severe problems, and this is particularly true of utterance gifts. We should learn from history, both biblical and secular, that to resort to gifts of the Spirit for guidance is to set a snare for ourselves, and to invite disaster.

Three rather prominent movements whose records are available for scrutiny — the Montanists, known as the "new prophecy" movement; the Irvingites of Great Britain; and the more recent Latter Rain movement — can trace their demise largely to misunderstanding and misuse of the gift of prophecy.*

The principal use of the gift of prophecy is forthtelling. However, it must be emphatically stated that ordinary preaching can in no way qualify as a manifestation of this gift. Prophecy, somewhat like preaching, is speaking forth; but in the case of prophecy, it is speaking forth with both supernatural impetus and Spirit-directed content. It is speaking with the force of heaven's authority; not in mere words of human wisdom, but in the power and demonstration of the Holy Ghost. It is not speaking the mere letter which kills, but speaking by the Spirit which gives life.

---

*For an enlargement of this subject, I suggest that the reader see my book *Charismatics, Are We Missing Something?* for a chapter entitled "Utterance Gifts for Guidance."

Only Spirit-filled persons truly prophesy. Peter, newly filled with the Spirit at Pentecost, prophesied so forcefully that 3,000 people were converted. And it is written of the Ephesian elders that **...the Holy Ghost came on them; and they...prophesied** (Acts 19:6).

A second function of the gift of prophecy is forthtelling, although this is far less common than forthtelling. Foretelling and fortune-telling are not to be confused. Fortune-telling is strictly forbidden by the Scriptures. Basically, God does not want us to know the future other than as it is revealed in His Word. The only sense in which knowing the future is justified is if it is of a redemptive nature and profitable for His Kingdom. Several such instances are recorded in the book of Acts. We will focus on them when we illustrate the manifestation of the gift of prophecy in the Early Church.

Both functions of this gift — forthtelling and foretelling — are encompassed in Paul's words to the Corinthians: **...he that prophesieth speaketh unto men to edification, and exhortation, and comfort** (1 Cor. 14:3). Any purported function outside these guidelines ought to be examined with great care.

Unlike the gifts we have already examined, for which biblical guidelines are somewhat minimal, there are several clearly stated directives for proper exercise of the gift of prophecy.

For instance, in Romans 12:6 Paul instructs: **...let us prophesy according to the proportion of faith.** For us to attempt to prophesy without active faith which unites us with the wellspring of true prophecy is to speak out of our own heart. It is this kind of false prophesying that offers the hearers "pie in the sky," and does not come to grips with reality. Listen to Jeremiah:

> **Thus saith the Lord of hosts, Hearken not unto the words of the prophets that prophesy unto you: they make you vain: they speak a vision of their own heart, and not out of the mouth of the Lord.**
>
> **They say still unto them that despise me, The Lord hath said, Ye shall have peace; and they say unto every one that walketh after the imagination of his own heart, No evil shall come upon you.**
>
> **Jeremiah 23:16,17**

Another guideline for those who prophesy is set forth in 1 Corinthians 14:29: **Let the prophets speak two or three, and let the other judge.** The *New International Version* puts it even more clearly: **Two or three prophets should speak, and the others should weigh carefully what is said.** In some quarters there is a prevailing misconception that prophesying is the exclusive province of preachers and spiritual leaders. However, Paul certainly speaks to that point when he says, **For ye may all prophesy one by one...**(1 Cor. 14:31). And again he says, **But if all prophesy, and there come in one that believeth not, or one unlearned, he is convinced of all, he is judged of all** (1 Cor. 14:24).

Some attention should be directed to the responsibility for judging what appears to be a prophetic utterance. It is the privilege and responsibility of those who hear to judge. It is not quenching the Spirit to judge, as some would have us believe. It is, in fact, quenching the Spirit when we do not obey the scriptural order.

But why judge a spiritual utterance? Can we not trust the Holy Spirit? Does the Holy Spirit make mistakes? The answer to all of these questions is quite simple. If the Holy Spirit were solely responsible and totally the agent, there would be no necessity whatever for judging. However, the infallible Holy Spirit must work and manifest His gifts through fallible human instruments. That is where the problem lies. Fallible men can easily fail to differentiate between that which springs from their own human spirits and that which is truly of the Spirit of God. They can experience genuine revelation from the Spirit of God on one hand, and on the other hand mingle it with their own earthly sentiments.

A case in point is Paul's experience at Tyre where he, while in a meeting with certain disciples, was directed through some form of spiritual utterance not to go to Jerusalem. When the details of the entire episode are carefully studied, it becomes apparent that Paul had determined, even before he began this particular journey, that he was in harmony with God's will in going to Jerusalem. Yet, he noted that at every stop-over ...**the Holy Spirit witnesseth..., saying that bonds and afflictions abide me** (Acts 20:23). Even after the experience at Tyre, when Paul reached Caesarea a prophet named Abagus ...**took Paul's girdle, and bound his own hands and feet, and said, Thus saith the Holy Ghost, So shall the Jews at Jerusalem bind the man that owneth this girdle, and shall deliver him into the hands of the Gentiles** (Acts 21:11).

And yet Paul went to Jersualem. Why? It appears on the surface that he almost flagrantly cast aside unmistakably clear warnings. But that is not the case. Paul was judging the prophecies which he had heard. He clearly understood that trouble awaited him, but he must have perceived also that the purely human sentiments of his brethren must not be allowed to interfere with his determination to **...know him (Christ)...and the fellowship of his sufferings, being made comformable unto his death** (Phil. 3:10).

Even so must we judge. The criterion is not to be mere human discretion, but it must always be the Word of God: **To the law and to the testimony: if they speak not according to this word, it is because there is no light in them** (Is. 8:20).

A further guideline for the exercise of the gift of prophecy is found in 1 Corinthians 14:32: **...the spirits of the prophets are subject to the prophets.**

We must not be deceived into believing that we simply lose control when God's Spirit comes upon us, and that we must speak forth regardless of the circumstances. The fact is that the truly Spirit-filled are in control of their own spirits and are able to move along within the biblical guidelines as the Spirit gently leads. The Holy Spirit never forces or pushes or compels. He leads. Thus we need never feel that we are under constraint beyond our own volition to speak forth; but, on the contrary, that we are privileged to do so, and we may.

The same principle applies to one who by the Spirit speaks in an unknown tongue. The spirit by which he speaks is subject to him, just as the spirit of the prophet is subject to the prophet: **But if there be no interpreter, let him keep silence in the church; let him speak to himself, and to God** (1 Cor. 14:28).

A final guideline for those who are gifted to prophesy is found in 1 Corinthians 14:37: **If any man**

think himself to be a prophet, or spiritual, let him acknowledge that the things that I write unto you are the commandments of the Lord. Perhaps the most important guideline of all for those who prophesy is the injunction that they maintain a proper spirit and attitude, and that they walk in humble obedience to Christ's commands. When this is done, how beautiful and effective is the manifestation of this gift.

Now, following the pattern already established as we have considered each of the gifts, we will seek to see how the gift of prophecy is exemplified in the ministry of Jesus, in the Early Church, and in contemporary experience.

Consider first the gift of prophecy in Jesus' ministry. Not only did Jesus prophesy, He was a prophet: **For Moses truly said unto the fathers, A prophet shall the Lord your God raise up unto you of your brethren, like unto me; him shall ye hear in all things whatsoever he shall say unto you** (Acts 3:22). It should be said here that all who prophesy are not prophets, in the sense of Ephesians 4:11; but it is also recognized that all who are truly prophets do prophesy. Thus prophecy must be recognized as a normal part of Jesus' ministry.

While it is not difficult to discover the foretelling aspects of His ministry, it is problematic to attempt to decide what aspect of Jesus' public utterance was not prophecy. Everywhere He is seen speaking forth with a unique authority: **For he taught them as one having authority, and not as the scribes** (Matt. 7:29). **The officers answered, Never man spake like this man** (John 7:46).

Also in keeping with our perception that the gift of prophecy encompasses a life-giving function, we are reminded again of Jesus' own declaration following the great discourse on the bread of life: ...**the words that I speak unto you, they are spirit, and they are life** (John 6:63).

The vast majority of Jesus' speaking forth was unto edification, exhortation and comfort, which is characteristic of the gift of prophecy. Luke records beautifully testimony to this truth: **And all bare him witness, and wondered at the gracious words which proceeded out of his mouth...** (Luke 4:22).

The gift of prophecy was quite common in the Early Church, being manifested through both the spiritual leaders and Spirit-filled lay people. Perhaps the outstanding example of its manifestation through a spiritual leader was the message Peter delivered on the day of Pentecost. His utterance that day was more than a prepared sermon. There was an authority in it, before unknown to Peter. Accompanying his utterance was a life-giving force that brought a host of his hearers into vital relationship with God. It is fair to say that Peter was speaking beyond himself, and that he demonstrated, at its epitome, the gift of prophecy. And it should be noted that both aspects of prophecy — forthtelling and foretelling — were present in his Spirit-inspired declarations.

The foretelling aspect of the gift of prophecy was in evidence in the Early Church on more than one occasion. An example is recorded in Acts 11:28: **And there stood up one of them named Agabus, and signified by the spirit that there should be great dearth** throughout all the world: which came to pass in the days of Claudius Caesar.

Before concluding our observations relating to the Early Church, we do well to remind ourselves once again of Peter's profound declaration as he himself was carried along by the gift of prophecy:

> **And it shall come to pass in the last days, saith God, I will pour out of my Spirit upon all flesh: and your sons and your daughters shall prophesy. . . .**
>
> **And on my servants and on my handmaidens I will pour out in those days of my Spirit; and they shall prophesy.**
>
> Acts 2:17,18

As if to indicate exact fulfillment of that prophecy, the record declares, through the words of Luke, the physician:

> **. . . and we entered into the house of Philip the evangelist, which was one of the seven; and abode with him.**
>
> **And the same man had four daughters, virgins, which did prophesy.**
>
> Acts 21:8,9

> **And when Paul had laid his hands upon them (that is, the Ephesian elders), the Holy Ghost came on them; and they spake with tongues, and prophesied.**
>
> Acts 19:6

It is my conviction that the gift of prophecy is more prevalent on the contemporary scene than is commonly recognized. Often it functions in the midst of ordinary preaching. Suddenly the preacher is carried along, as if by a rushing wind, and he finds himself uttering truth not found in his notes nor springing from his previous meditation, and yet so profound and powerful as to mightily affect his hearers and cause them to sense that they are hearing from God.

Even apart from preaching, the gift of prophecy is being manifested through godly lay people who, under the direction of the Holy Spirit, speak forth words of edification, exhortation and comfort — words which bear their own good fruit both within the Body itself and in the lives of unbelievers.

However, rather than attempting to illustrate this occurrence, I encourage the reader to be on the alert for manifestation of the gift, and to personally prepare his or her heart so that he or she may be a channel through whom the gift can be freely manifested.

Notes

[1] Donald Gee, *Spiritual Gifts in the Work of the Ministry Today* (Springfield, Missouri: Gospel Publishing House, 1963), p. 43.

[2] James Strong, S.T.D., LL.D., *Strong's Exhaustive Concordance of the Bible*, "Greek Dictionary of the New Testament," entry –3056, (Nashville: Abingdon, 1978), p. 45.

[3] Ibid., entry –4487, p. 63.

[4] Harold Horton, *The Gifts of the Spirit*, 10th. ed. (Nottingham, England: Assemblies of God Publishing House, 1971), p. 167.

[5] Dennis and Rita Bennett, *The Holy Spirit and You* (S. Plainfield, NJ: Bridge Publishing, Inc., 1971), p. 99. Reprinted by permission of the publisher.

[6] Donald Gee, *Concerning Spiritual Gifts* (Springfield, Missouri: Gospel Publishing House), p. 42.

[7] L. Thomas Holdcroft, *The Holy Spirit, A Pentecostal Interpretation* (Springfield, Missouri: Gospel Publishing House, 1962, 1971, 1979), p. 167.

12

Discerning of Spirits

...to another discerning of spirits....

1 Corinthians 12:10

My first very real confrontation with the spirit world came when, as a young man, I was attending North Central Bible College in Minneapolis, Minnesota. Since the college was in its earliest stages of development, it did not yet have dormitories. Most of us students were housed in private homes. Several of us rented rooms on the upper floor of a large dwelling on Chicago Avenue.

The owners of the house were members of the Minneapolis Gospel Tabernacle, where the Bible college classes met. They had one son, Les, who also attended North Central.

Quite often we students who lived in the home would assemble in one of the rooms for a time of prayer. While we were praying together on a certain evening, Les was sitting at the piano downstairs rehearsing a lesson.

"Les, why don't you join the boys in prayer this evening?" his mother questioned.

"Oh, Mother," he responded, "I have this piano lesson which I must practice, and I have other studies which I must do. I just don't have time."

So Les went on practicing. And we continued praying. Nevertheless, in a few minutes he left the piano, mounted the stairs, and entered the room where we were engaged in earnest prayer.

No word was exchanged between us, but the moment Les entered, it seemed as if all hell broke loose. An awesome sense of prevading darkness enveloped us. Virtual terror seemed to fasten upon us. So fearful was the confrontation that I ran to the stairway landing and called to Les' mother, asking her counsel on how we should handle the frightening situation.

"Plead the blood of Jesus," she admonished, "and continue praying."

Following her direction, in a matter of minutes we found the darkness had fled away, like a wild beast before a hunter, and an overwhelming sense of glorious triumph filled our hearts. Even so, none of us really understood the experience, nor did we know what to make of the strange encounter.

A week later Les was chapel speaker. He spoke like a veteran. His message was clear and inspiring. As he neared his conclusion, he related the strange experience of the week before. He told of sitting at the piano while we prayed, of how his mother had urged him to join us, of how he had responded that he just didn't have time, of how a moment later he felt strongly impressed to join us, of how he had ascended the stairs and entered the room where we were praying and of the fearsome and strange struggle which had ensued. And he concluded the account by joyfully announcing: "That night God delivered me from a thing I had battled for two years."

The simplest explanation I have is that that night we did battle in the spirit world and by the grace of God won a great victory. To God be the glory!

As we begin our study of the gift of discerning of spirits, we should take note that in this gift, as in all others, various aspects of God's nature are brought into the limelight. We need but look when it is manifested, and we will see God.

The stage is set for our study by Jesus' forthright declaration: **God is a Spirit**...(John 4:24). That is fundamental to our understanding, for who can know the spirit world like God Who Himself is a Spirit? We as humans are beset with limitations, but God is unlike mortal man. He is not a physical being. Jesus said, **...a spirit hath not flesh and bones**...(Luke 24:39). And because God is not a physical being, He is not subject to the limitations imposed by flesh and blood. While man *has* a spirit, God *is* a Spirit.

Being a Spirit, then, and knowing none of the confinements imposed by flesh and blood, He has that great quality called omnipresence, which gives Him total awareness at all times and of all worlds — the spirit world included.

We do well to ponder the wonders of omnipresence, for I think we suffer great loss when our eyes are dim to this glorious reality. A. W. Tozer is exceedingly helpful when he says: "Canon W. G. Holmes of India told of seeing Hindu worshippers tapping on trees and stones, and whispering, 'Are you there? Are you there?' to the god they hoped might reside within. In complete humility the instructed Christian brings the answer to that question. God is indeed there. He is there as He is here and everywhere, not confined to a tree or stone, but free in the universe, near to everything, next to everyone, and through Jesus Christ immediately accessible to every living heart. The doctrine of divine omnipresence decides this forever."[1]

Yes, God is a Spirit, and thus He is endowed with omnipresence, not merely because He is a Spirit, but because He is God. Certainly all spirits are not omnipresent. Peter speaks to this point when he says of Jesus, **...he went and preached unto the spirits in prison** (1 Pet. 3:19). And again, speaking of the angels who sinned, he says that they were **...delivered...into chains of darkness, to be reserved unto judgment** (2 Pet. 2:4).

Not only is God a Spirit, but as has been noted previously, He is the Father of spirits: **...shall we not much rather be in subjection unto the Father of spirits, and live?** (Heb. 12:9). Commenting on this passage, *The Pulpit Commentary* states: "...it is not human spirits only that are here in the writer's view. God is the Father of all 'the spirits,' whether in the flesh or not; all are of Divine parentage, for God himself is Spirit."[2]

Along with understanding that God is the Father of all spirits, we must also understand that all spirits are not godly. It is for this very reason that the gifts of discerning of spirits is of such great consequence. More attention will be given later to the whole spectrum of the spirit realm. However, for the moment it will be helpful to consider God's awareness and knowledge of the entire spirit world.

God knows all spirits. Since He is both omnipresent and omniscient, all spirits are always in

His range of seeing and knowing: **Neither is there any creature that is not manifest in his sight: but all things are naked and opened unto the eyes of him with whom we have to do** (Heb. 4:13).

Therefore, when the gift of discerning of spirits is manifested, the Holy Spirit simply draws on the vast reservoir of God's omnipresence and omniscience and applies it on the human scene.

By why is discerning of spirits necessary? Why should believers covet such a gift? What good purpose could it serve? There are numerous answers to these questions, but a single answer comprehends them all. There is a very real spirit world. That world has in it elements that are bent on destruction: destruction of every believer, destruction of every segment of the true Church, destruction of all that is moral and good and righteous, and even destruction of the world itself. In John 10:10 Jesus uncovered the mission of this evil spirit realm: **The thief cometh not, but for to steal, and to kill, and to destroy. . . .** Through discerning of spirits, the believer is enabled to identify these destructive spirits so that they may be dealt with properly and defeated.

Examining the spirit world from a biblical perspective, we discover essentially four kinds of spirits:

1. Foremost among spirits is God Himself, as has already been discussed.

2. Angels, too, are identified as spirits: **But to which of the angels said he at any time, Sit on my right hand, until I make thine enemies thy footstool? Are they not all ministering**

spirits, sent forth to minister for them who shall be heirs of salvation? (Heb. 1:13,14).

3. Again, the Bible speaks of the spirit of man, or the spirit in man: **For what man knoweth the things of a man, save the spirit of man which is in him?...(1 Cor. 2:11). ...and I pray God your whole spirit and soul and body be preserved blameless...**(1 Thess. 5:23).

4. Finally, it speaks of evil spirits and of an evil spiritual realm: **And in that same hour he cured many of their infirmities and plagues, and of evil spirits...**(Luke 7:21). **For we wrestle not against flesh and blood, but against principalities, against powers, against the rulers of the darkness of this world, against spiritual wickedness in high places** (Eph. 6:12).

Discerning of spirits has to do primarily with this last order of spirits — evil spirits and wicked spiritual entities. However, it may also function in discerning of the Spirit of God, or the spirit of man, for there are instances wherein man by his own judgment may attribute to Satan that which is actually a work of the Holy Spirit, and likewise some may attribute to the Holy Spirit that which springs from the human spirit.

But, I repeat, the gift of discerning of spirits has primarily to do with evil spirits, and with wicked spiritual entities.

The reality of such spiritual beings ought not to be considered lightly. Careful attention to the Gospels reveals that a great facet of Jesus' ministry was the exorcising of evil spirits. Could it be that many of the problems of our time, both in and out of the Church, are traceable to evil spirits? Indeed, it may well be, for we are confronted with a whole spiritual world.

These beings fasten themselves to human beings, oppressing, obsessing and possessing. They seek to bind the preacher, blind the hearer and pervert the truth. They seduce; they lie; they bind; they hinder; they incite to lust and all manner of evil; they smite with fear; they generate illness and infirmity; they promote unbelief and evil imagination; they withstand the Gospel ministry. And, if I may say it, they do all of this, and much more, often scarcely without being recognized for who they are. Thus we conclude that discerning of spirits is a much needed gift for today.

This gift requires thoughtful definition, since its function is so important, and also since an accurate perception of its function will provide a sound base for the faith necessary to its meaningful manifestation.

The word *discern* itself provides valuable help in understanding the gift. It means "looking beyond the outward to the inward" (literally, "seeing right through").

L. Thomas Holdcroft says of the gift: "The Holy Spirit manifests the gift of discerning of spirits to enable the believer to form judgments and recognize entities in the realm of spirits. The term *discerning* (lit., discernings) in the original connotes a judgment made possible by an insight that sees through externals and perceives basic underlying reality. . . . By means of this gift, human natural senses are supplemented by appropriate divine powers, so that humans are able to relate in understanding in the spirit world. The gift of discerning of spirits does not enable one to discern people; it is not 'discernment' in the abstract, but simply what it purports to be: the discerning or analytic classification and judgment of spirits."[3]

Insights provided by G. Raymond Carlson are also very worthy of note: "This manifestation has nothing to do with E.S.P. Nor does this come through training, but it is given in a moment when and as it is needed. It is not by keen insight into human nature such as a psychiatrist may have. Thus it is not human shrewdness, character reading, fault finding, or thought reading. Nor is it natural discernment of humans, nor even spiritual discernment (1 Corinthians 2:14).

"The real nature of this gift is knowing and judging, but never guessing. It is to know what is in a person and to know the spirit. The Church is guarded against evil spirits and deceivers, and they are exposed."[4]

Since one of my great concerns is to aid the Body of Christ in seeing God in each of the gifts, I add my own definition:

The gift of discerning of spirits is the supernatural impartation of a bit of God's own perception of spirits, springing from His omnipresence and His omniscience, to a believer, by the Holy Spirit, whereby spirits manifesting or seeking to conceal themselves are known for exactly what they are.

Understanding is always aided and elevated by illustration. Consequently we once again resort to the ministry of Jesus, to the Early Church and to contemporary experience for actual accounts of the effective operation of this gift.

Interestingly enough, our first illustration is drawn from a face-to-face confrontation which Jesus had with His own disciples. The Samaritans of a certain city had refused to receive Jesus:

> And when his disciples James and John saw this, they said, Lord, wilt thou that we command fire to come down from heaven, and consume them, even as Elias did?
>
> But he turned, and rebuked them, and said, Ye know not what manner of spirit ye are of.
>
> Luke 9:54,55

This is most certainly not grounds for believing that James and John were at that point possessed by an evil spirit, but it seems evident that they were playing into Satan's hand, becoming tools for destruction rather than instruments of mercy. Therefore Jesus said, "Ye know not what spirit ye are of." He had discerned the spirit to which they had momentarily given way.

Another event in Jesus' ministry effectively demonstrates the gift of discerning of spirits as it was manifested in connection with a most remarkable healing. A woman appeared in the synagogue where He was teaching on the Sabbath. She was pitifully bent over, and had been in that state 18 long years. In His great compassion, Jesus called her to Him and said:

> ...Woman, thou art loosed from thine infirmity.
>
> And he laid his hands on her: and immediately she was made straight, and glorified God.
>
> Luke 13:12,13

Reading on in the account, it becomes evident that Jesus had discerned an evil spirit of infirmity as the root of the problem, for in answering the ruler of the synagogue, who was indignant over His healing on the Sabbath, Jesus asked, **And ought not this woman, being a daughter of Abraham, whom Satan hath bound, lo, these eighteen years, be loosed from this bond on the sabbath day?** (Luke 13:16).

Again the record indicates that Jesus discerned an evil spirit influencing Peter on a certain occasion: **But he turned and said unto Peter, Get thee behind me, Satan: thou art an offence unto me...**(Matt. 16:23).

It is not difficult to trace this gift in the Early Church. By discerning of spirits Peter knew that Ananias and Sapphira had surrendered to a lying evil spirit: **But Peter said, Ananias, why hath Satan filled thine heart to lie to the Holy Ghost...?** (Acts 5:3).

Elymas the sorcerer provides another illustration. Sergius Paulus, deputy of the isle of Paphos, had desired to hear the Word of God from Paul. But Elymas, who was also a Jew and a false prophet, contested with Paul, trying to dissuade the deputy from the faith. On the surface it may have appeared to the unlearned that here was a confrontation between two Jewish prophets. However, Paul, by the Holy Ghost, saw right through his opponent. He discerned the evil spirit possessing and using the man, and with eyes ablaze with holy disdain, he said, **...O full of all subtilty and all mischief, thou child of the devil, thou enemy of all righteousness, wilt thou not cease to pervert the right ways of the Lord?** (Acts 13:10).

Nor does the account end until by another of the Spirit's gifts Paul has pronounced blindness "for a season" upon the instrument of Satan.

A final example from the Early Church is recorded in Acts 16. Paul and Silas were in Philippi. En route to a prayer meeting, possibly in the house of Lydia, a seller of cloth, a young lady joined with those gathering to pray. No doubt the believers detected something strange about her, but as Paul and his company moved about, she seemed always to be there. And often she must have interrupted his moving about with an ecstatic utterance.

Most who heard her must have said, "What a prophetess she is," for she cried out, . . .**These men are the servants of the most high God, which shew unto us the way of salvation** (Acts 16:17). This was her constant message — and what she said was true. I have wondered what would happen if one like her appeared in some of our American churches. Is it possible we would offer her our pulpits?

Not Paul. He . . .**turned and said to the spirit, I command thee in the name of Jesus Christ to come out of her. And he came out the same hour** (Acts 16:18).

What a classic illustration of the gift of discerning of spirits.

Steve Ziemke was remarkably converted from the drug culture in 1971 and shortly thereafter was baptized in the Holy Spirit.

Three weeks after his conversion, he met a friend who also had been in the drug culture. When Steve testified to him of his recent experience in receiving Christ as his personal Savior, his friend indicated that he, too, had left the drug scene.

Responding to his friend's invitation, Steve accompanied him to his church. Together they attended a Bible class and the morning service. Being a young Christian, Steve didn't detect anything seriously wrong in what he heard; yet deep within his being he was made aware of a strange spirit present in the meeting. By his intellect he was unable to identify or sort out any particular error. But to his spirit, the Holy Spirit unmistakably flashed a warning that he was surrounded by a spirit of error.

After Steve had shared his strange experience with his mother he discovered that his friend had taken him to a cultist meeting place.

Truly the Holy Spirit had given Steve the very meaningful gift of discerning of spirits whereby he experienced that which is set forth in 1 John 2:26,27:

These things have I written unto you concerning them that seduce you.

But the anointing which ye have received of him abideth in you, and ye need not that any man teach you: but as the same anointing teacheth you of all things, and is truth, and is no lie, and even as it hath taught you, ye shall abide in him.

Notes

[1]A. W. Tozer, *The Knowledge of the Holy* (New York: Harper & Row, 1961), p. 81.

[2]The Rev. J. Barmby, B.D., *The Pulpit Commentary on Hebrews* (London and New York: Funk and Wagnalls Company), p. 357.

[3]L. Thomas Holdcroft, *The Holy Spirit, A Pentecostal Interpretation* (Springfield, Missouri: Gospel Publishing House, 1962, 1971, 1979), p. 150.

[4]G. Raymond Carlson, *Spiritual Dynamics* (Springfield, Missouri: Gospel Publishing House, 1976), pp. 102,103.

13

Divers Kinds of Tongues

...to another divers kinds of tongues.

1 Corinthians 12:10

Carrie Judd Montgomery was a devout and dedicated Christian. Her name is revered around the world. To begin our study of the gift of tongues and to set the stage for our adventure into this intriguing subject, I will quote two affidavits relating to this remarkable woman, giving the full text of each. The first is from Mrs. Montgomery herself, and the other is from Harriette M. T. Shimer who had some association with Mrs. Montgomery and who gives testimony to what she vouched.

"Soon after receiving the fullness of the Holy Spirit in June, 1908, I was filled with a remarkable love for the Chinese people. There had been in my heart a great interest in them for many years, but this was something different — an outgoing of the Spirit in divine love toward them, and intercession which was wonderful. I had been speaking in several different 'tongues,' some of which sounded like the languages of India, but about this time I was conscious of speaking another language which seemed like Chinese.

"As time went on a number of different Chinese people who heard me speaking assured me that I was talking in Chinese. I was led to ask the Lord to raise up a credible witness, for the glory of God, to verify this Chinese language, if such it was.

"At Beulah Park, Ohio, this past summer, I met Mrs. Harriette Shimer, a missionary of the Society of Friends, who had been working in China for the past seven years. This dear sister did not know much about the Pentecostal work, and was opposed to what she had heard of it. She was interested, however, after I told her of my personal experience. I invited her to stay that evening to a little meeting in an upper room, where we had arranged to pray for some hungry souls. She accepted this invitation.

"The meeting was very quiet and the power and presence of God pervaded the room in a wonderful way. Presently Mrs. Shimer heard someone singing in Chinese, and opened her eyes to see who it could be. She was amazed to find it was myself through whom the Spirit was giving utterance in this way. I perceived upon her countenance conflicting emotions, great awe, consternation and bewilderment. So troubled did she look that in the midst of the singing I smiled at her to make her know that all was well. She said afterwards that this smile did much to reassure her, for she saw I was not unconscious or in a trance, but in perfect possession of all my senses.

"As it was too late after the meeting for Mrs. Shimer to return to her home in Cleveland, I offered to share my room and bed with her. We slept quietly for three or four hours, then both became wide awake. The sweet melting power of the Lord was upon me, and His music was in my innermost soul, and it welled up in song (not loud enough to disturb other sleepers near) in a language that did not sound to me like the Chinese. Mrs. Shimer, however, assured me that I was singing another Chinese dialect to one of the tunes often heard in China. The manifestation again seemed so marvelous as to produce a degree of fear in this dear sister and she asked if she could light the lamp to look at me, to which I consented. She placed her hand upon me and made the remark that my flesh was soft and warm and not rigid and cold, as she supposed it might be under such extraordinary manifestations. As soon as her fear was removed this dear one (who had been sweetly taught of God in the past) began to recognize the presence and power of God which brooded over us both, and to yield to it herself, so that her own soul began to receive great blessing. The rest of the night at intervals I sang and talked Chinese in different dialects which she recognized, but toward morning she said, 'You have not yet spoken in Mandarin, which is my dialect.' I replied, 'I will ask the Lord to let me speak in the Mandarin,' to which she answered, 'No, I have had all I can stand for one night!'

"The next morning we were gathered again in a precious little meeting, when I began to sing in the Mandarin at which Mrs. Shimer suddenly interrupted me with, 'Do you know what you are saying?' and gave the interpretation. After this again and again the Spirit gave utterance in the Mandarin, which of course, was always easily translated by Mrs. Shimer, as she said that I spoke it much more perfectly than she could, although she had been in the country seven years. Sometimes the most difficult Chinese songs were reproduced note by note with mighty ascriptions of praise to God. Sometimes the soul of this dear sister was so melted by the power of the message that she wept, and sometimes she was so filled with heavenly joy that she laughed with delight. Twice the Lord gave me interpretation before she could translate it, and in each instance the interpretation was verified by Mrs. Shimer.

"It is impossible for me to describe the great joy and the adoration to God which accompanies these manifestations of the Spirit's indwelling. When so many are yielding themselves to the enemy that he may use their lives and their lips to carry out his evil purposes, how blessed it is to feel one's self a channel for the divine Spirit to flow through and speak through as He will."

Mrs. Shimer has written the following in corroboration of the above:

"I desire to testify to what I have recently witnessed of the wonderful power of God as manifested in the Gift of Tongues. At a late Christian Alliance convention, I met some Spirit-filled women who had received this gift, and in a prayer meeting which was held for the healing of some sickness, I heard Mrs. Carrie Judd Montgomery of Oakland, California, praying in the Chinese language. I could readily understand her, because of my years of mission work in China.

"Some weeks following this convention it was my privilege to be much associated with Mrs. Montgomery, and she repeatedly prayed and sang in Chinese, the tunes themselves sometimes being distinctly Chinese.

"My astonishment at this marvelous working of God was not greater than the joy that came to me at the quickening of my own spiritual life through this experience. Previous to this I had been much pre-judiced against what is known as the Pentecostal movement, but through God's direct teaching and leading I cannot but believe that God is ready to bestow the fullness of His Holy Spirit, and this Pentecostal gift of tongues upon His wholly surrendered children. So I am constrained by my love and loyalty to Him to give this testimony, that others prejudiced as I was may be encouraged to take God at His word and press on to receive all of His fullness."

Every gift of the Holy Spirit, including the gift of divers kinds of tongues, casts its own peculiar rays of light on the being of God, and is indeed a profound disclosure of some glorious aspect or aspects of His wondrous Self.

While the human mind will never totally sort out all of the mystery surrounding this gift, we can be assured that the Scriptures do provide adequate understanding of our present need.

It is fair to begin with the assumption that all languages have their roots in God Who has revealed Himself as the Great Communicator. The record indicates that even before mankind was on the scene communication transpired at the level of the Godhead: **And God said, Let us make man in our image, after our likeness...**(Gen. 1:26). Furthermore, it is clear that original man, made in the image of his divine Creator, was likewise endowed with communicative abilities. It is extremely doubtful that Adam had to learn the language he spoke. As we have previously surmised, Adam was likely the first human to be given a language supernaturally. If we understand the account correctly,

God had hardly finished His masterpiece — man — when He began communicating with him: **And the Lord God commanded the man, saying...**(Gen. 2:16). **And they** (Adam and Eve) **heard the voice of the Lord God...**(Gen. 3:8).

Evidence indicates that from Adam to Babel a common language prevailed: **And the Lord said, Behold, the people is one, and they have all one language...**(Gen. 11:6). Philologists may disagree, endeavoring to show from their findings "that the existing differences of language changes were brought about by the operation of natural causes, such as the influence of locality in changing and of time in corrupting human speech.

"But (1) modern philology has as yet only succeeded in explaining the growth of what might be called sub-modifications of human speech, and is confessedly unable to account for what appears to be its main divisions into a Shemitic, an Aryan, and a Turanian tongue, which may have been produced in the sudden and miraculous way described (in Gen. 11:7); and (2) nothing prevents us from regarding the two events, the confusion of tongues and the dispersion of nations, as occurring simultaneously, and even acting and reacting on each other. As the tribes parted, their speech would diverge, and, on the other hand, as the tongues differed, those who spoke the same or cognate dialects would draw together and draw apart from the rest."[1]

The point we wish to make is that at Babel God Himself confounded their common tongue by establishing in its place a diversity of tongues. And it seems evident that not only did men receive and speak new languages, they also received the ability to understand those new languages. That is, each group spoke and understood only the particular tongue it had received. The source of the new tongue, and of the ability to understand that new tongue, was God. While this is hardly equatable with the New Testament gift of tongues and interpretation, it does illustrate the idea of languages, and the understanding of those languages, being imparted by supernatural means.

Somewhat amusing is the record of Balaam's donkey speaking supernaturally: **And the Lord opened the mouth of the ass, and she said unto Balaam, What have I done unto thee, that thou hast smitten me these three times?** (Num. 22:28). There is but a single explanation for this strange account. The Great Communicator caused the mute animal to speak.

In each of these instances God is the fountainhead of the supernatural communication. The same may be said of Daniel in his encounter with Belshazzar when words in an unknown language appeared upon the palace walls: "Mene, Mene, Tekel, Upharsin." (Dan. 5:25.) Those were words direct from God. And only one person, Daniel, was gifted by God to interpret them.

One thing is certain. With God there is no hidden language, no uncracked code, no mysterious hieroglyphics. He needs no interpreter and no Rosetta stone.* All languages, whether the tongues of men

---

*"A piece of black basalt found in 1799 near the Rosetta mouth of the Nile, bearing a bilingual inscription (in hieroglyphics, demotic characters, and Greek), and famous as having given M. Champollion the first clue toward deciphering the Egyptian hieroglyphics."[2]

or the tongues of angels, are totally at His command, and it is out of this unlimited reservoir that the gift of divers kinds of tongues emerges. Thus when the gift is manifested in its purity, we are honored with a glimpse of the Great Communicator.

"Divers kinds of tongues" must never be construed to mean learned languages or languages known to the speaker. The language may well be a known language as at Pentecost: **And how hear we every man in our own tongue, wherein we were born?** (Acts 2:8). Or it may even be a language totally foreign to earth: **Though I speak with the tongues...of angels...** (1 Cor. 13:1). In all cases, with no exception, true tongues-speaking is by the enablement of the Holy Spirit: **And they...began to speak with other tongues, as the Spirit gave them utterance** (Acts 2:4). Paul wrote: **...I will pray with the spirit, and I will pray with the understanding also...** (1 Cor. 14:15). The inference is clear: "When I pray with the spirit (that is, in tongues), even I do not understand the language by which I am praying."

How important is this gift? For a long time now we have been told that tongues is the least of the gifts, and therefore hardly worthy of our attention. However, the exact opposite seems nearer the truth. If tongues are of little value, and if they are only for the spiritually immature (as some would assert), why does Paul make so much of them? Why does he say, **I would that ye all spake with tongues...** (1 Cor. 14:5)? And further, why does he testify, **I thank my God, I speak with tongues more than ye all** (1 Cor. 14:18)?

Thankfully a new day has dawned for tongues-speaking. It is practiced by millions the world over, and yet I fear the Church has not fully grasped the vital meaning of the gift.

Consider several key reasons for its significance. Perhaps highest on the list is the gift's enhancement of the worship experience. **. . .the Father,** Jesus told us, **seeketh such to worship him** (John 4:23); that is, **. . .they that worship him. . .in spirit and in truth** (v. 24). It is doubtful if worship in the spirit ever rises higher and glorifies God more than when one worships in tongues. It was this unparalleled worship by those newly filled with the Spirit that gripped the attention of the onlookers on the day of Pentecost, causing them to cry out: **. . .we do hear them speak in our tongues the wonderful works of God** (Acts 2:11).

Ivar A. Frick, Assemblies of God District Superintendent for Michigan, tells that when his son, Larry, and his wife were ministering to some tribal people in Kenya, East Africa, they heard someone praising God in perfect English. Realizing that the language of the people was Swahili, Larry sought out the person who was speaking so beautifully. She was a black woman, totally ignorant of the English language. With tears streaming down her ebony face, and with a glow that only Deity could impart, she was exalting Christ in a language totally foreign to her. It should be said here that there is no better way to worship God than in the Spirit through the gift of tongues.

The gift of tongues is extremely significant as it relates to prayer. Who has not sensed deep within his spirit the need for some special enablement whereby he may be more effective before the throne of grace? Tongues is the answer. Paul testified, "I will pray with the spirit." (1 Cor. 14:15.) Again he taught, **He that speaketh in an unknown tongue edifieth himself...** (1 Cor. 14:4). And to the Romans he wrote, **Likewise the Spirit also helpeth our infirmities** (that is, our feeblemindedness in knowing what to pray for)**; for we know not what we should pray for as we ought: but the Spirit itself maketh intercession for us with groanings which cannot be uttered** (Rom. 8:26).

If the gift of tongues was significant for no other reason than as an aid to prayer, that would be enough to make it extremely important and meaningful to every believer.

The gift of tongues serves a significant role in relation to other gifts of the Spirit. It paves the way for supernatural manifestations, both by being the means whereby the believer is himself spiritually built up, and by generating the faith by which other gifts operate. We are reminded that when large diesel engines were first used, they were very difficult to start. To handle this problem, some companies mounted small gasoline engines alongside their diesel engines, purely as starting devices. Similarly, it can be said that tongues is the "starter gift." In the book of Acts it was the first gift to appear, and it set the stage for all to follow.

Most of us have difficulty moving into the supernatural. We are so hamstrung by our humanity. Nevertheless, the gift of tongues can provide the extra boost we need.

A special feature relating to the gift of tongues is that it is available to every believer. Not one person need feel that tongues are not for him — Paul's question, **...do all speak with tongues?...** (1 Cor. 12:30), not withstanding. Yes, there will be those who will not be employed by the Holy Spirit in manifesting the gift in public service. But until there is a single person who does not need special enablement to pray effectively, until there is a child of God who can reach the ultimate of worship apart from the Holy Spirit's help, everyone may and should speak in tongues.

Tongues, it may be said, is the language of the spirit. It enables highest communication of spirit with Spirit — of man and his Maker. Montanus described this beautiful spiritual exercise: "Each human spirit is like a harp, which the Holy Spirit strikes with a plectrum and which yields itself to the mighty hand by which the chords are swept."[3]

Moving through the book of Acts and the first epistle to the Corinthians, we get a picture of tongues-speaking in various settings and under a variety of circumstances. On the day of Pentecost, man first began experiencing this phenomenon, and the Scriptures indicate it was a direct result of his having been filled with the Holy Ghost: **And they were all filled with the Holy Ghost, and began to speak with other tongues, as the Spirit gave them utterance** (Acts 2:4).

From my perspective, this first occurrence serves as a distinctive precedent for the Church Age. I am aware that there are some scholars who hold a somewhat different view. For example, one author says, "There is no express teaching as to...any specific charismatic phenomena that are to be in evidence when one receives the Spirit...it does not say that

Christians are to be baptized in the Spirit evidenced by tongues."[4]

While we must agree that there are no such verbal declarations, we must strongly insist that there is "express teaching," for teaching is accomplished wherever there is learning, regardless of the presence or absence of certain verbalizing.

That such "express teaching" did occur cannot be doubted when the Cornelius experience is evaluated. Peter's criterion for evaluating the Gentile experience was what he had been taught by the initial outpouring of the Spirit:

> **For they heard them speak with tongues, and magnify God. Then answered Peter,**
>
> **Can any man forbid water, that these should not be baptized, which have received the Holy Ghost as well as we?**
>
> **Acts 10:46,47**

There is a third recorded instance of tongues-speaking in Acts. It happened while Paul was in a meeting with a few disciples in Ephesus. Upon inquiring, Paul learned that they were totally ignorant of the Holy Ghost: **...We have not so much as heard whether there be any Holy Ghost** (Acts 19:2). Then, after having taught them and led them into water baptism, he **...laid his hands upon them; (and) the Holy Ghost came on them; and they spake with tongues, and prophesied** (Acts 19:6).

It should be noted that in each instance of tongues-speaking in Acts, it had to do with initial reception of the Holy Spirit. Some hold the view that this was not the gift of tongues to which Paul refers in 1 Corinthians 12-14. "The baptism of believers in the Holy Ghost is witnessed by the initial physical sign of speaking with other tongues as the Spirit of God gives the utterance (Acts 2:4). The speaking in tongues in this instance is the same in essence as the gift of tongues (1 Corinthians 12:4-10,28) but different in purpose and use."[5]

Not a great deal is to be gained from debate over what is or is not the gift of tongues, for such debate usually has more to do with semantics than with the vital issues. One thing is certain. Tongues-speaking does serve several purposes:

1. It is the initial physical evidence that one has indeed been filled with the Spirit. (Acts 2:4.)

2. It may be a sign for the unbeliever. (Acts 2:7-12; 1 Cor. 14:22.)

3. It brings edification to the person who so speaks. (1 Cor. 14:4.)

4. It is a force for edification of the Church when interpreted. (1 Cor. 14:5.)

5. It is an effective prayer device. (1 Cor. 14:14,15; Rom. 8:26; Eph. 6:18; Jude 20.)

Our principal concern in this chapter is the function of the tongues gift in the public service. It is this function which is in view, and to which Paul is addressing himself in 1 Corinthians 12-14. Understanding this, we come nearest to correctly understanding Paul's question, "Do all speak in tongues?" (1 Cor. 12:30.) He is addressing himself to functioning of gifts (particularly the utterance gifts) "in the church" and in behalf of the Body, and is not likely at all mindful of the initial reception of the Spirit. No, all do not exercise the gift in the public service. Yes, all should expect to speak with tongues when filled with the Spirit.

The essential purpose for the tongues gift in the public service is edification of the Body of Christ: **...seek that ye may excel to the edifying of the church** (1 Cor. 14:12).

Early in 1 Corinthians 14, Paul makes an evaluation of the two gifts — tongues and prophecy — as forces for edifying the Church. Several points should be noted: In verse 1 he says, **...but** (desire) **rather that ye may prophesy.** This statement has been taken to mean that prophecy is the greatest of all the gifts. However, in consideration of the context it appears much more accurate to assume that Paul's intention was to compare tongues and prophecy, rather than prophecy and all other gifts, for in verse 5 he says, **I would that ye all spake with tongues, but rather that ye prophesied....** The obvious reason for this preference is that tongues-speaking by itself edifies only the speaker, while prophecy edifies the whole Body.

It does appear very doubtful that a speaker in tongues could be edified by a "message" intended for the congregation if it was not interpreted; but, on the other hand, it seems most reasonable that an individual speaking unto God in a tongue in worship, prayer or praise would most certainly be edified.

To go on with the comparison, Paul calls attention to a difference between the two gifts:

> **For he that speaketh in an unknown tongue speaketh not unto men, but unto God....**

But he that prophesieth speaketh unto men....
1 Corinthians 14:2,3

Admittedly, this is a troublesome passage for it seems to set the direction for the two gifts — tongues toward God, and prophecy toward men. While an increasing number of Pentecostal scholars espouse this view, there are others who find difficulty in so interpreting this passage.

Some hold that the statement, "For he that speaketh in an unknown tongue, speaketh not unto men but unto God," simply means that only God understands the mysteries spoken in a tongue, and that the statement is not intended to convey the idea that the utterance is positively directed toward God.

For example, Dr. Stanley Horton, a highly respected Assemblies of God scholar, states: "The reason that one speaking in tongues is not talking to men while he is speaking in tongues is that no one present understands what is being said except God. There is nothing in this verse to rule out tongues being addressed to men."[6]

On the other hand, Dr. Gordon Fee, another widely recognized Assemblies of God scholar, takes quite the opposite view. He writes: "Such a person is 'speaking to God', that is, he or she is communing with God by the Spirit. Although it is quite common in Pentecostal groups to refer to a 'message in tongues', there seems to be no evidence in Paul for such terminology. The tongues-speaker is not addressing fellow believers but God (cf. vv. 13-14,28), meaning therefore that Paul understands the phenomenon basically to be prayer and praise."[7]

It is of special interest, and, I think, of no small consequence, that so able a scholar as G. Campbell Morgan, who, although not a Pentecostal and could therefore be credited with great objectivity, stated: "That is the first great truth to be remembered, that the gift of tongues was for addressing God. It was not for addressing men. It was never given in order that men might preach.

To put it quite simply, in our everyday language it was given to men that they might praise. These voices, these tongues, were utterances of ecstatic gladness, in adoration and in praise. Tongues were given, and they were to be used in addressing God."[8]

The two statements in verses 2 and 3, "speaketh not unto men, but unto God," and "speaketh unto men," seem to be somewhat superfluous if they were not intended to indicate the object toward which the speaking was addressed.

Dr. Fee, identified above, observes: "With two balanced pairs (vv. 2-3) Paul first contrasts tongues and prophecy as to who is addressed...and therefore as to their basic purpose...; the second pair (v. 4) then interprets the first pair in terms of who is being edified. Thus:

"For

"a) The one who speaks in tongues speaks
              not to people,
              but *to God*.

          Indeed, no one understands him;
          he speaks mysteries by the Spirit.

194

"On the other hand,
"b) The one who prophesies speaks to people,
  edification,
  encouragement,
  comfort.

"Paul's emphasis — and concern — is unmistakable, the edification of the church. The one activity, tongues, edifies the speaker but not the church because it is addressed to God and 'no one understands him.' The other activity, prophecy, edifies the church because it is addressed to people and speaks 'edification, encouragement and comfort' to them."[9]

Also contributing to our understanding is Paul's employment of the Greek ou, which the *King James Version* translates "not" in the statement "speaketh *not*." According to E. W. Bullinger in *The Companion Bible, ou* means "expressing full and direct negation, independently and absolutely, not depending on any condition expressed or implied."[10] Thus it seems evident that Paul was wishing to underscore and emphasize the point that one speaking in tongues was indeed addressing God, and not men.

Another related problem centers on Paul's statement, "howbeit in the spirit he speaketh mysteries." To rightly understand what he meant by "mysteries" is to understand also the object toward whom the tongues-speaking is addressed.

Stanley Horton feels rather strongly that "mysteries" confirms the idea that tongues may contain a message for men. He states: "That the tongues contained something for men is further confirmed by the fact that they are mysteries spoken by the Spirit.

Paul usually used the word 'mystery' to express something hidden in Old Testament times but is now revealed in the gospel. Mysteries then are secret truths revealed by God to men. They impart the wisdom of God (1 Corinthians 2:7)."[11]

Fee, on the other hand, understands "mysteries" in another way. He comments: "The content of such utterances is 'mysteries' spoken 'by the Spirit.' It is possible that 'mysteries' means something similar to its usage in 13:2; more likely it carries here the sense of that which lies outside the understanding, both for the speaker and the hearer. After all, 'mysteries' in 13:2 refers to the ways of God that are being revealed by the Spirit to His people; such 'mysteries' would scarcely need to be spoken back to God."[12]

I personally lean toward this latter view.

First Corinthians 14:5,6 is also a point of controversy. At first glance verse 5 seems to indicate that tongues, when interpreted, is equal to prophecy, and in such usage would be in the form of a message from God to men. However, from my perspective, it is not accurate to think that Paul intended for us to understand that he was dealing with either the content of the utterance or the object toward which it was aimed. Rather he was addressing himself to comparative force for edification, and he was simply saying, "The man who prophesies is a greater force for edification of the Church than is he who speaks in a tongue, unless he interprets."

Horton seems to concur, for he states: "Some commentators take v. 5 to mean tongues with interpretation are equivalent of prophecy in all respects.

Others rightly object. This verse by itself does not imply that they are exact equivalents, but only that both edify the Church."[13]

And Fee agrees: "The interpretation of the tongue brings it within the framework of intelligibility, which in turn means that it too can edify the community. This does not imply that such a tongue is to be understood as directed toward the community but that what the person has been speaking to God has now been made intelligible, so that others may benefit from the Spirit's utterance."[14]

Verse 6 certainly bears heavily on the question of whether or not tongues is intended to convey a message from God to men. Horton holds that "whether they (that is, prophecy and interpreted tongues) are equivalent or not depends on how the next verse (v. 6) is interpreted."[15] And we heartily agree.

However, Horton rises immediately to support the view that verse 6 does indeed indicate the content of interpreted tongues. He writes: "Actually, the word 'now' is better translated 'since this is so,' in other words, since tongues should be interpreted to edify the Church. The thought is, *'If I come to you speaking in tongues, how will I benefit you unless I speak (that is, by the gift of interpretation) either in revelation or in knowledge, or in prophecy or in teaching?'* The intent is clearly that the tongues when interpreted can bring these benefits."[16]

Fee, on the other hand, views verse 6 from a somewhat different perspective. He comments: "A turn in the argument is indicated both by the vocative 'brothers (and sisters)' (see on 1:10) and by the conjunctive combination 'but as it is.' This opening sentence functions as a transition. It carries forward the argument of vv. 1-5; at the same time it sets the stylistic pattern for the first set of analogies ('If . . . , how shall . . .?'), which argue vigorously against unintelligibility (=tongues) since it has no usefulness for its hearers.

"Even though the sentence is probably intended to present a hypothetical setting for the argument, both the combination 'but as it is' and the language 'if I come to you' support the suggestion made above that this is more than merely hypothetical; probably it also indicates the way things presently are between them and him, implying his rejection of their criterion for being *pneumatikos* ('spiritual'). Paul in effect refuses to 'come to (them) speaking in tongues.' The reason for this echoes the motif of edification from vv. 3-5. By following their criterion he would not 'profit them.'

"The alternative is for him to come speaking some form of intelligible utterance, which he illustrates with yet another list of *charismata*. This list is both illuminating and intriguing. On the one hand, the appearance of prophecy in the third position intimates, as has been argued in vv. 1-5, that the real issue is not tongues and prophecy as such, but tongues and intelligibility, for which prophecy serves as the representative gift. On the other hand, as with the other lists in this argument, this one is also especially *ad hoc*. His concern is to specify various kinds of Spirit-inspired utterances that have intelligibility as their common denominator. Thus he includes two items from previous lists, 'knowledge' and 'prophecy' (see 12:8-10; 13:2,8). The other two call for additional comment.

"Despite our lack of certainty about the precise nature and content of these various forms of utterance, however, their common denominator is their intelligibility, and to that question Paul now turns in the form of analogies."[17]

While the above material may be a bit weighty and technical, Fee seems to understand that verse 6 does not project the content of interpreted tongues, but rather Spirit-inspired utterances of various kinds, by which the Church may be edified.

Viewing verse 6 in the light of its broad context, this author espouses the view that Paul was not intending to say that tongues interpreted might take the form of a "revelation," a word of "knowledge," a "prophecy," or a "doctrine," but rather that he was urging that space be given for other manifestations, in addition to tongues and interpretation, for the edification of the Church.

As I have indicated in my book, *Charismatics, Are We Missing Something?*, I sincerely feel that there may be an area of truth we Pentecostals tend to overlook — that tongues is essentially a prayer and worship gift and that its primary function is not a "message" from God to the Church, but rather it is a Spirit-inspired utterance toward God. I urge that our best Pentecostal scholars give more serious study to this matter. If we have somehow overlooked a meaningful truth, we need to know it. If, on the other hand, our traditional view is accurate, we need to know that too.

I am well aware that experience and certain biblical interpretation would tend to negate the idea that tongues-speaking in the public service is essentially toward God. For so long we have had our "messages" in tongues and interpretations directed toward the congregation. And there are recorded instances wherein individuals have spoken in tongues unknown to themselves and yet known to someone present, and the tongue was in the form of a message to the one who understood; but I must say that this latter type case is extremely rare. And it is possible that when this does happen, it may well not be the regular function of tongues but rather a manifestation of the gift of miracles or a co-mingling of the two.

Some believers question how utterances in tongues directed toward God could possibly edify the Church. My personal observation is that no utterance in tongues and interpretation has ever edified me more than those directed to God. The late Earl W. Goodman, a man of intense spiritual perception, often interpreted tongues in my hearing, and invariably it was in the highest praise and exaltation of the Father and the Son.

Through the gift of prophecy, the edification of the Body springs from words of edification, exhortation and comfort, and it is possible that much of what we perceive to be interpretation is more technically prophecy. Not that it matters to God, except that by our misunderstanding we may be missing another means of edification springing from being able to say the "amen" to glorious worship, praise, prayer, thanksgiving and blessing of God which results from true interpretation of tongues.

Much more needs to be said on this subject, and much more objective study and research needs to be forthcoming. However, for now let it suffice to say that our common concern must be that the gift of tongues may be manifested most meaningfully and most biblically. In the meantime, let us be yielded vessels through whom the Holy Spirit can manifest this beautiful gift, and let us be guided by our best understanding of the gift, so that the Church can be edified.

Before concluding our study of this gift, we must give a bit of attention to the biblical guidelines for its manifestation in the Church:

1. Tongues must not be given too much prominence: **Now, brethren, if I come unto you speaking with tongues, what shall I profit you, except I shall speak to you either by revelation, or by knowledge, or by prophesying, or by doctrine?** (1 Cor. 14:6). While some construe this verse to indicate possible content of an utterance in tongues, I take Paul to mean, as I have already stated, that we need to make room for more than tongues-speaking.

2. Utterances in tongues are to be limited as to number in a given service: **If anyone speaks in a tongue, two — or at the most three — should speak, one at a time, and someone must interpret** (1 Cor. 14:27 NIV). We need to remember that Paul is speaking to the cause of edification. While he may not condemn utterances beyond the two or three limit, he sees that the Church is best edified by the imposed limits.

3. Utterances in tongues must be interpreted: **...if there be no interpreter, let him keep**

silence in the church; and let him speak unto himself, and to God (1 Cor. 14:28). Responsibility for interpretation rests first with the speaker in tongues. Unless he himself is gifted to interpret, before speaking in a tongue in the public service, he must know that one gifted as an interpreter is present. He is also to heed the instruction, **...let him that speaketh in an unknown tongue pray that he may interpret** (1 Cor. 14:13).

4. Tongues-speaking is not to be forbidden: **...forbid not to speak with tongues** (1 Cor. 14:39).

5. Effort must be put forth to avoid confusion: **Let all things be done decently and in order** (1 Cor. 14:40).

Now, since the gift of tongues was not present in Jesus' ministry, being for some reason especially reserved for the Church Age, and since it is difficult to illustrate its function in the Early Church, we will conclude our study with several helpful definitions, and with only contemporary illustrations.

G. Raymond Carlson says: "Speaking in tongues is expressing words one has never learned, but which are communicated by the Holy Spirit....The gift of tongues can be public prayer (1 Corinthians 14:13-16). The interpretation can be petition, praise, or thanksgiving."[18]

"Speaking with tongues," says Harold Horton, "is supernatural utterance by the Holy Spirit in languages never learned by the speaker — not understood by the mind of the speaker — nearly always not understood by the hearers. It has nothing whatever to do with linguistic ability, nor with the mind or intellect of man. It is a manifestation of the mind of the Spirit of God employing human speech organs."[19]

To these I add my own definition:

The gift of divers kinds of tongues is supernatural ability, given to the believer by the Holy Spirit, to speak in either earthly or heavenly languages wholly unknown to himself, for his own personal edification, for edification of the Church, or for a sign to the unbeliever.

A beautiful illustration of this gift was given to me by the late Glenn M. Horst, once pastor of Full Gospel Tabernacle of Gary, Indiana. I quote him verbatim:

"The Sunday before Easter of 1950, in the Full Gospel Tabernacle of Gary, Indiana, a Mrs. Novak spoke in a language that she did not understand. She was scarcely seated until one of the men of the church, whom I recognized to be an Italian, stood to his feet and excitedly said: 'She is speaking my language. I understood everything she said.'

"I replied, 'What did she say?'

"This man gave the interpretation of what Mrs. Novak had just spoken: 'O King Eternal, Thou art our King Eternal! Lead on, King. Withersoever Thou leadest us, we will follow Thee. If Thou leadest us through the valleys deep, or if Thou leadest us up to the mountains steep, withersoever Thou wilt lead us, we will follow Thee. Lead on, O King Eternal, lead on.' "

A final testimony is from W. F. P. Burton, former missionary to the Congo, now deceased:

"Twice I have heard Kiluba spoken by Spirit-filled believers in England. This is a Central African language, and Sister Durham and Donald Gee, who spoke it, had no opportunity of learning it. It was in joy and praise to the Lord Jesus.

"During one of our Mwanze Bible Conferences we were waiting on the Lord and some were praying very earnestly to be endued with power from on high. A young man, named Saiba, was praying quietly with eyes shut, when I noticed that his lips were moving rapidly. Going behind him, I was amazed to find that he was telling of the glories of Christ's coming Kingdom in a language of which he did not understand a word.

"I cannot describe the awe with which I realized that this miracle was straight from God for me. His language was perfect. He was telling of Jerusalem, the center of Christ's earthly reign, of the fruitfulness and peace that should flourish, of the nations bringing their glory and wealth to an earthly and to a heavenly city, of there being no further necessity for guns or explosives, warships or armored trains.

"Oh, the tenderness with which he spoke of Christ's righteousness and inflexible justice, of His ruling over those for whom He once shed His life's blood.

"It may have been 10 minutes, or perhaps 20, that I listened spellbound. Later I asked him if he knew what he had said. He answered that he just knew that he had been glorifying in the wonders of the Lord Jesus. His spirit was praying, but his understanding was unfruitful. Certainly some of the truths that he uttered concerning Christ's millennial reign were truths which he himself had never known before."

Notes

[1]*The Pulpit Commentary on Genesis* (London and New York: Funk and Wagnalls Company), p. 166.

[2]*Webster's New Collegiate Dictionary* (Springfield, Mass.: G. & C. Merriam Co., Publishers, 1975), p. 736.

[3]The Very Rev. F. W. Farrar, D.D., *The Pulpit Commentary of 1 Corinthians* (London and New York: Funk and Wagnalls Company), p. 457.

[4]Gordon D. Fee and Douglas Stuart, *How To Read The Bible For All Its Worth* (Grand Rapids: Zondervan Corporation, 1981), p. 100. Used by permission.

[5]General Council of the Assemblies of God, *Minutes and Revised Const. and Bylaws* (1981), p. 93.

[6]Stanley Horton, as quoted in *Paraclete* (magazine published by the Assemblies of God, Springfield, Missouri), Spring 1980.

[7]Gordon Fee, *The New International Commentary on the New Testament* (First Epistle to the Corinthians) (Grand Rapids: Wm. B. Eerdmans Publishing Co., 1987), pp. 656, ppg. 1.

[8]G. Campbell Morgan, *The Corinthian Letters of Paul* (Old Tappan, NJ: Fleming H. Revell Co.), p. 169, ppg. 2.

[9]Fee, p. 655, ppg. 2.

[10]E. W. Bullinger, *The Companion Bible*, appendix 105, as quoted in Dialogue (magazine published in McLean, Virginia), Mar./Apr. 1988, p. 4.

[11]Horton, p. 25, ppg. 6.

[12]Fee, p. 656, ppg. 2.

[13]Horton, p. 27, ppg. 6.

[14]Fee, p. 659, ppg. 1.

[15]Horton, p. 27, ppg. 6.

[16]Ibid., p. 28, ppg. 3.

[17]Fee, p. 661, ppgs. 2,3; p. 662, ppg. 1; p. 663, ppg. 2.

[18]G. Raymond Carlson, *Spiritual Dynamics* (Springfield, Missouri: Gospel Publishing House, 1976), p. 105.

[19]Horton, p. 141.

14

Interpretation of Tongues

...to another the interpretation of tongues.

1 Corinthians 12:10

Early in January 1961, Dr. Thomas F. Zimmerman, former General Superintendent for the Assemblies of God, was guest speaker at a minister's meeting in Alton, Illinois. As he was ministering in a Wednesday night service, an unusual move of the Holy Spirit swept over the congregation, and a layman, Cloyd McCleery, gave an utterance in an unknown tongue. This was followed by an interpretation by Dr. Zimmerman.

Following a volume of prayer and praise which arose from the congregation, a Mrs. Anna Richards Scoble requested permission to speak. Greatly broken and deeply moved, she stated that a marvelous miracle had just occurred. She explained that Cloyd had spoken in a language of the Transvaal in Southern Africa.

She went on to further explain that she had been a missionary in the Transvaal for 47 years, and that she herself spoke the language. She said that the utterance had been spoken perfectly through the Spirit, despite the fact that foreigners find it most difficult to master some parts of the language. For an example, she cited the word for God, stating that it could not be pronounced correctly, except by nationals. She declared that Mr. McCleery had enunciated every word with exactly the right voice inflections.

Concluding her remarks, Mrs. Scoble affirmed that Dr. Zimmerman's interpretation had been correct in every detail.

Interpretation of tongues is but another reflection of the being of our infinite God. To Him in Whom all communication has its base, interpretation is the natural thing. He requires no linguistic specialist, nor the assistance of modern technology. At once, all language is at His complete command.

We marvel at humans who master a number of languages, and we may credit them with genius, but our God is the Source of all language and of interpretation of all communication. Interpretation is a most natural demonstration of omniscience.

Therefore, when interpretation of tongues occurs, we do well to remind ourselves that once again we are glimpsing the God to Whom alone interpretation belongs.

To aid us in understanding the function of this gift, we will look to several able scholars for their definitions.

"The function of the gift of interpretation of tongues," according to L. Thomas Holdcroft, "is not a mental performance, but a spiritual process. It is not so much that one deliberately and consciously analyzes what he has heard, but rather that he submits to the Holy Spirit to allow him to communicate as he sees fit."[1]

G. Raymond Carlson states: "As a manifestation of the Spirit, vastly superior to human thought and volition, this gift may be defined as an inspired explanation in commonly understood language of an inspired utterance in tongues. As the utterance when speaking in tongues is not conceived in the mind, so the utterance of interpretation proceeds from the Spirit rather than from the intellect of the person."[2]

According to Harold Horton, "Interpretation of tongues is the supernatural showing forth by the Spirit of the meaning of an utterance in other tongues. This interpretation is not an operation of the mind of the interpreter but the mind of the Spirit of God. The interpreter never understand the tongue he is interpreting, and it is no part of his task to provide equivalent terms in his own tongue for the supernatural words spoken. They are unknown words: so much so that they are quite indistinguishable in the phrases of which they form a part. The interpretation is just as much a miracle as the original utterance in tongues. Both are utterly equally direct from the mind of the Spirit of God."[3]

For a final definition other than my own, we look to the late R. M. Riggs: "Interpretation of tongues has nothing to do with the interpretation of Scripture.... Interpretation of tongues is a supernatural gift, like the gift of tongues or the gift of miracles. It is entirely dependent upon the gift of tongues and has no function apart from that gift. It is in reality an interpreting or giving the sense of that which has been spoken in the gift of tongues."[4]

My own definition:

The gift of interpretation of tongues is a supernatural impartation of God's own interpretative ability to a believer, whereby he is enabled to state the meaning of an utterance in tongues in such a way that those who are present may understand and thus be edified.

It should be understood that interpretation of tongues is not translation of tongues. Translation is the process whereby effort is made to give the exact equivalent of a given language in another language. On the other hand, interpretation, while not an attempt to provide the exact equivalent of a given language, is a means for giving the general meaning of what has been spoken.

The Scriptures provide some rather clearcut guidelines for proper use of this gift:

1. The speaker in tongues is to pray that he may interpret: **Wherefore let him that speaketh in an unknown tongue pray that he may interpret** (1 Cor. 14:13). The rather obvious reason for this directive is that tongues-speaking apart from interpretation does not edify the Body of Christ. Interpretation provides the means whereby the entire Body can benefit.

2. There is a strong inference that if a person prays or sings in tongues in the public service, his praying or singing should be interpreted: **Else** (that is, unless accompanied by interpretation) **when thou shalt bless with the spirit, observes Paul, how shall he that occupieth the room of the unlearned say Amen at thy giving of thanks, seeing he understandeth not what thou sayest? For thou verily giveth thanks well, but the other is not edified** (1 Cor. 14:16,17).

   While some do not think that Paul was addressing himself to interpretation of tongues in verse 16, but rather to praying and singing merely from one's own mind and in one's own language, the context seems to indicate otherwise.

The key word is the preposition "for" at the beginning of verse 14, which ties the directive to verses 14 and 15: **For if I pray in an unknown tongue, my spirit prayeth, but my understanding is unfruitful. What is it then: I will pray with the spirit, and I will pray with the understanding also: I will sing with the spirit, and I will sing with the understanding also.** Thus I perceive Paul to be saying, "Pray that you may interpret, because when you pray in an unknown tongue you don't understand what you are praying. So pray and sing in a tongue, but pray that you may interpret what you have prayed, and that you may interpret what you have sung, so that those present who do not understand will be able not only to understand but to say 'amen' to what you have said and what you have sung, and thus be edified."

A few years ago at Glacier Bible Camp (just west of Glacier National Park) a large family camp was in session. On a certain evening the congregation was engaged in a joyous worship time. Suddenly someone in the audience sang out in a tongue. There was a beautiful poetic rhythm to the utterance. But the delight of all who heard it was greatly heightened when the minister leading the worship time sang out an interpretation with the identical poetic rhythm. What a glorious edification!

3. For each utterance there should be a single interpretation: **...and let one interpret** (1 Cor. 14:27). It could be inferred from this guideline that one person should interpret all of the utterances, whether there be one, two or three. However, it seems more reasonable to believe that the intention is, let one person interpret each utterance, rather than, let one person interpret all utterances. One factor supporting this view is the previous instruction that the person giving an utterance is to pray that he may interpret. Thus, if three different people gave successive utterances, it is not unreasonable to believe that each of those three persons would interpret his own utterance.

The most important concern seems to be that for each utterance there is to be only a single interpretation. More than one interpretation for a single utterance, occurring simultaneously, would certainly violate the rule, "Let all things be done decently and in order," and might also generate additional confusion by any variance in the interpretations.

4. A final guideline, applying not only to interpretation of tongues, but to all of the utterance gifts in particular, is the directive, **...seek that ye may excel to the edifying of the church** (1 Cor. 14:12).

Uppermost must be the motivation of love, a sincere desire to edify the Body and to glorify God. And when this is the case, even the unbeliever will not have good reason to **...say that ye are mad...** (1 Cor. 14:23).

As with the gift of tongues, there is no illustration of interpretation of tongues in the ministry of Jesus. Nor is there any positive illustration of it from the Early Church, although some have supposed that the message recorded in Acts 21:4 **(...who said to Paul through the Spirit, that he should not go up to Jerusalem)** was given in the form of tongues and interpretation. My personal view is that the evidence for supporting such a perception is entirely too flimsy. There is little biblical justification for personal guidance through utterance gifts.

For our final illustration I have chosen an account provided by Amelia Bullock, a person with more than average linguistic ability. Please note carefully how her understanding of what was spoken in a tongue unknown to the speaker was in harmony with the interpretation given:

"I had recently been saved in an Assembly of God church. I was not willing to leave the Greek Orthodox church for it had been the faith of my parents and forefathers for generations.

"I had planned to attend the Greek Orthodox church on Sundays, the Assembly of God church on week days, but a young people's rally changed my life forever. During the service, Mother Flower (Mrs. J. Roswell Flower) gave an utterance in tongues in French concerning the second coming of the Lord. Having studied several languages, with the intention of becoming a linguist, I was able to translate what she spoke before the interpretation was given. I found it agreed with my translation! Surely this was of God!

"Fear gripped m :. I vowed before the Lord that if He would baptize me with the Holy Spirit and cause me to speak in a tongue I would step out of the Greek Orthodox church and join hands with the Pentecostals.

"Five days later I received the Holy Spirit and spoke in other tongues."

Notes

[1] L. Thomas Holdcroft, *The Holy Spirit, A Pentecostal Interpretation* (Springfield, Missouri: Gospel Publishing House, 1962, 1971, 1979), p. 165.

[2] G. Raymond Carlson, *Spiritual Dynamics* (Springfield, Missouri: Gospel Publishing House, 1976), p. 106.

[3] Harold Horton, *The Gifts of the Spirit*, 10th ed. (Nottingham, England: Assemblies of God Publishing House, 1971), p. 156.

[4] Ralph M. Riggs, *The Spirit Himself* (Springfield, Missouri: Gospel Publishing House, 1949), pp. 166,167.

15

From the Meeting Place
to the Marketplace

There is a most interesting contrast between the final verse of Luke's Gospel and the final verse of Mark's Gospel. Speaking of Jesus' disciples, Luke indicates that they **...were continually in the temple, praising and blessing God...** (Luke 24:53); but Mark states that they **...went forth, and preached every where, the Lord working with them, and confirming the word with signs following...** (Mark 16:20). The message is clear — both the meeting place and the marketplace are vital to the advancement of God's Kingdom.

The meeting place is essentially for worship and edification. The marketplace is for evangelization. The meeting place is for ministry to the saints. The marketplace is for ministry to the lost.

In the meeting place men are to be endued with the power of God; in the marketplace men are to minister by the power of God.

The burden and primary message of this book has been gifts for the marketplace. Our purpose has been to generate a greater awareness of the need for and possibility of manifestation of the Spirit's gifts outside the four walls of the sanctuary. Awareness of God in the meeting place ought always to result in awareness of God in the marketplace.

Yet the disquieting question is: How can this really happen? How can we see more gifts of the Spirit manifested on "main street"? How can we apply any new understanding we may have gleaned relating to the Spirit's gifts where it will truly count for the Kingdom?

First of all, by awareness. Awareness is the launching pad for action. For so long, I fear, we have been quite unaware that the gifts of the Spirit could have a meaningful role in the marketplace. If we did have any such awareness at all, we made little of the idea. We were so content with what gifts, if any, were manifested in the meeting place, that we gave no thought to the marketplace. But now it is different. Now we are aware of the vast new possibilities.

Awareness itself opens doors. While ministering in a large church in Ohio during the summer of 1984, I saw this truth beautifully demonstrated. I had been teaching on the Spirit's gifts, much as I have shared in this book. On a certain day I had ministered in a morning session, explaining the function of the word of wisdom and establishing an awareness of its availability through the Holy Spirit.

One of those present was the church's full-time, well-trained counselor. At the time of the evening service the same day, he came to me excitedly telling of an incident which had taken place that very afternoon.

He had been counseling with someone and had reached an impasse. He had exhausted all of his resources in an effort to help his client, but was aware that he was unable to resolve the problem. Quietly opening his heart to the Lord, in a moment he was given a word of wisdom, not his own, that met the need perfectly and sent his counselee on his way rejoicing.

A second vital step toward the enabling of marketplace manifestations is reviving the almost lost practice of waiting on God. I know of no more important action. Someone has wisely observed that when *we* work, God waits; but when we wait, *God* works. This is not to say that we ought to do no work; but when we seek to go to the marketplace without having waited upon God, we are unwittingly saying that we can do it alone. Waiting upon God develops an inward confidence and an expectation necessary to the Spirit's manifestation.

Waiting on God prepares us for what God has prepared for us: **For since the beginning of the world men have not heard, nor perceived by the ear, neither hath the eye seen, O God, beside thee, what he hath prepared for him that waiteth for him** (Is. 64:4).

There is both a time to wait and a time to act: **And the Lord said unto Joshua, Get thee up; wherefore liest thou thus upon thy face?** (Josh. 7:10).

The Spirit's gifts can find no expression through us in the marketplace until *we* are found in the marketplace. As the Early Church went forth preaching, they witnessed the signs following.

A final important step is making oneself available to the Spirit, and being sensitive *toward* the Spirit:

> **And the angel of the Lord spake unto Philip, saying, Arise, and go toward the south unto the way that goeth down from Jerusalem unto Gaza, which is desert.**

And he arose and went....

Then the Spirit said unto Philip, Go near, and join thyself to this chariot.

And Philip ran....

Acts 8:26,27,29,30

"O Lord, stir us to go to the marketplace — outside the walls of our beautiful churches, into the court room, into the city streets, inside prison walls, onto the mission field, onto the road where lonely men walk, into the bedroom of the afflicted, into the morgue, into the humble abode of wayfaring men and into the penthouses of the elite. Help us to go wherever men are in need.

"And as we go, enable us by the might of thy Holy Spirit to be channels for His mighty gifts, whereby our desperately needy world shall be helped.

"Amen."

Bibliography

Barmby, The Rev. J., B.D. *The Pulpit Commentary on Hebrews*. London and New York: Funk and Wagnalls Company.

Bennett, Dennis and Rita. *The Holy Spirit and You*. S. Plainfield, NJ: Bridge Publishing, Inc., 1971.

Blaikie, The Rev. Professsor W. G., D.D. *The Pulpit Commentary on Ephesians*, Wartime edition. London and New York: Funk and Wagnalls Company.

Brandt, R. L. *Charismatics, Are We Missing Something?* Plainfield, NJ: Logos International, 1981.

Carlson, G. Raymond. *Spiritual Dynamics*. Springfield, Missouri: Gospel Publishing House, 1976.

Dialogue. McLean, Virginia: March/April 1988.

Farrar, The Very Rev. F. W., D.D. *The Pulpit Commentary on 1 Corinthians*, Wartime edition. London and New York: Funk and Wagnalls Company.

Fee, Gordon. *The New International Commentary on the New Testament*. Grand Rapids: Wm. B. Eerdmans Publishing Co., 1987.

Fee, Gordon D. and Stuart, Douglas. *How To Read The Bible For All Its Worth*. Grand Rapids: Zondervan Publishing House, 1981.

Gee, Donald. *Concerning Spiritual Gifts*, 10th ed. Nottingham, England: Assemblies of God Publishing House.

Gee, Donald. *Spiritual Gifts in the Work of the Ministry Today.* Springfield, Missouri: Gospel Publishing House, 1963.

General Council of the Assemblies of God. *Minutes and Revised Const. and Bylaws.* 1981.

Hedman, Jan. "I Was Sure I Must Pray," *Mountain Movers.* Springfield, Missouri: Gospel Publishing House, May 9, 1984.

Holdcroft, L. Thomas. *The Holy Spirit, A Pentecostal Interpretation.* Springfield, Missouri: Gospel Publishing House, 1962, 1971, 1979.

Horton, Harold. *The Gifts of the Spirit,* 10th ed. Nottingham, England: Assemblies of God Publishing House, 1971.

McRae, William. *Dynamics of Spiritual Gifts.* Grand Rapids: Zondervan Publishing House, 1976.

Morgan, G. Campbell. *The Corinthian Letters of Paul.* Old Tappan, NJ: Fleming H. Revell Co.

Palma, Anthony D. *The Spirit-God in Action.* Springfield, Missouri: Gospel Publishing House, 1974.

Paraclete. Springfield, Missouri: Assemblies of God, Spring 1980.

Plotts, Morris. *Bwana Tembo.* Baton Rouge, Louisiana: Jimmy Swaggart Evangelistic Assn., 1980.

Riggs, Ralph M. *The Spirit Himself.* Springfield, Missouri: Gospel Publishing House, 1949.

Smail, Thomas, A. *The Forgotten Father.* Grand Rapids: William B. Eerdmans Publishing Co., 1980.

Strong, James. *Strong's Exhaustive Concordance of the Bible*. Nashville: Abingdon Press, 1978.

The Pulpit Commentary on Genesis. London and New York: Funk and Wagnalls Company.

The Scofield Reference Bible. New York: Oxford University Press, 1909, 1917, 1937, 1945.

The Zondervan Parallel New Testament in Greek and English. Grand Rapids: Zondervan Publishing Company, 1980.

Tozer, A. W. *The Knowledge of the Holy*. New York: Harper & Row, 1961.

Webster's New Collegiate Dictionary. Springfield, Mass.: G. & C. Merriam Co., Publishers, 1975.

Additional copies of this book, plus other books by the author, may be obtained by writing to:

R. L. Brandt
1520 Westwood Dr.
Billings, MT 59102

Books available are:

Gifts for the Marketplace ....$ 6.95
Charismatics, Are We Missing Something?.............4.95
Praying with Paul 3.95
One Way...2.50

Please add $1.00 per book for handling and shipping. Write for postage rates if ordering more than three books. Discounts are available to book stores.

About the Author

R. L. Brandt served pastorates in North Dakota and Montana for nearly 17 years. For seven and one-half years he was National Home Missions Secretary for the Assemblies of God. He served the North Dakota and Montana districts of the Assemblies of God as District Superintendent for a combined total of nearly 20 years.

From his conversion as a farm boy, at age 16, until the present, he has had a vital interest in biblical teaching relating to the Holy Spirit, the gifts of the Spirit and related subjects. He has addressed congregations around the world, and has written extensively on these and other subjects.

He is a graduate of North Central Bible College, Minneapolis, Minnesota, and in 1985 was awarded an honorary Doctor of Divinity degree by Northwest College in Kirkland, Washington.